COACH BILL BELICHICK

AN UNAUTHORIZED LOOK
UNDER THE HOODIE

Dear Coach Bill Belichick,

As your self-proclaimed number one fan,
I hope we can meet one day without me finding myself
at the receiving end of a strongly-worded cease
and desist letter from your legal team.

Coach Bill Belichick
An Unauthorized Look Under the Hoodie

ISBN 979-8-9899482-8-4
Copyright © 2024 by Clay Clark

Thrive Publishing
Published by Thrive Publishing
3920 W 91st St S, Tulsa, OK 74132

Thrive Publishing books may be purchased for educational, business, or sales promotional use. For more information, please email the Special Markets Department at info@Thrive15.com.

CONTENTS

WHO IS CLAY CLARK?

Welcome to the start of your success story. Discipline is the bridge between dreams and accomplishment. Remember it's hard to build a reputation based on what you intend to do. Let's go dominate and get stuff done.

CLAY CLARK

Clay Clark is the former U.S. SBA Entrepreneur of the Year, Co-Host of the ThriveTimeShow.com Radio Show, the founder of Thrive15.com, and holds the self-proclaimed title as "Belichick's Number One Fan." Over the course of his career, he has been a founding team member of many successful companies including DJConnection. com, EITRLounge.com, MakeYourLifeEpic.com, Thrive15.com, and EpicPhotos.com (Dallas, Oklahoma City, etc.). He and his companies have been featured in Forbes, Fast Company, Entrepreneur, PandoDaily, Bloomberg TV, Bloomberg Radio, the Entrepreneur On Fire Podcast, the So Money Podcast with Farnoosh Torabi, and on countless media outlets. He's been the speaker of choice for Hewlett-Packard, Maytag University, O'Reilly Auto Parts, Valspar Paint, Farmers Insurance, and countless other companies. He is the father of five kids and he is the proud owner of 38 chickens, six ducks, four cats, and two Great Pyrenees dogs (at last count). Clay is an obsessive Coach Bill Belichick fan and Tim Tebow apologist. In honor of Coach Bill Belichick, Clay Clark wears a hoodie every day. When not chasing his kids and wife around, he enjoys reading business case studies and autobiographies about successful entrepreneurs.

February 21, 2007

Mr. Clayton Thomas Clark
DJ Connection Tulsa, Inc.
8900 South Lynn Lane Road
Broken Arrow, Oklahoma 74102

Dear Mr. Clark:

Congratulations! You have been selected as the **2007 Oklahoma SBA Young Entrepreneur of the Year**. On behalf of the U.S. Small Business Administration (SBA), I wish to express our appreciation for your support of small business and for your contributions to the economy of this State.

In recognition of your achievement, **an awards luncheon will be held Tuesday, May 22, 2007** at Rose State College in Midwest City, Okla. The luncheon is sponsored by the Oklahoma Small Business Development Center. Two complimentary luncheon tickets have been reserved for you and one guest.

Arrangements for the luncheon are still being finalized. You will be notified of the details as soon as they become available. You are encouraged to bring family, friends, and business associates. Upon presentation of your award, you will have the opportunity to make acceptance comments.

Also, for our awards brochure, please email an electronic photo of yourself to darla.booker@sba.gov by Friday, March 16.

Again, congratulations on your outstanding accomplishment.

Sincerely,

Dorothy (Dottie) A. Overal
Oklahoma District Director

As the man who is self-proclaimed as "Coach Bill Belichick's number one fan" I believe it is my civic duty for you and all Americans to know the epic 102 Coach Bill Belichick essential facts found in this book.

COACH BILL BELICHICK'S LEGENDARY FOOTBALL COACHING CAREER HIGHLIGHTS:

Through his 24 seasons in the NFL, Coach Bill Belichick won 17 AFC East titles, made 13 AFC Championship appearances, and nine Super Bowl appearances.

PLAYING CAREER:

1971–1974: Coach Bill Belichick played both Center and Tight End for the Wesleyan Cardinals. I believe it would be a strong marketing move for Wesleyan to put their pride aside & rename their team the Wesleyan Belichicks.

COACHING CAREER:

- » 1975: Baltimore Colts
- » 1976: Detroit Lions
- » 1977: Detroit Lions
- » 1978: Denver Broncos
- » 1979: New York Giants
- » 1980-1984: New York Giants
- » 1985 - 1990: New York Giants (DC)
- » 1991 - 1995: Cleveland Browns
- » 1996: New England Patriots
- » 1997 - 1999: New York Jets
- » 2000 - 2023: New England Patriots
- » 2025: North Carolina

AWARDS, HONORS & ACCOMPLISHMENTS:

As a head coach, Coach Bill Belichick has won six Super Bowls (XXXVI, XXXVIII, XXXIX, XLIX, LI, LIII).

As an assistant coach, Coach Bill Belichick has won two Super Bowls (XXI, XXV)

As a head coach, Coach Bill Belichick has received the following honors:

» 3× AP NFL Coach of the Year (2003, 2007, 2010)

» Maxwell Club NFL Coach of the Year (2007)

» NFL 2000s All-Decade Team

» NFL 2010s All-Decade Team

» NFL 100th Anniversary All-Time Team

» New England Patriots All-2000s Team

» New England Patriots 50th Anniversary Team

» New England Patriots All-2010s Team

» New England Patriots All-Dynasty Team

As an executive, Coach Bill Belichick received the Pro Football Weekly Association's Executive of the Year in 2021.

COACH BILL BELICHICK HOLDS THE FOLLOWING NATIONAL FOOTBALL LEAGUE RECORDS:

- » Most Super Bowl wins: 8
- » Most Super Bowl wins as a head coach: 6
- » Most Super Bowl appearances: 12
- » Most Super Bowl appearances as a head coach: 9
- » Most playoff wins as a head coach: 31
- » Most playoff appearances as a head coach: 19 (tied)
- » Most divisional championships as a head coach: 17

WILLIAM STEPHEN BELICHICK was born on the glorious day of April 16th, 1952. William "Bill" Belichick is a legendary American football coach who is currently the head football coach at the University of North Carolina at Chapel Hill. Many Coach Bill Belichick fans have begun calling the University, "University of North Carolina at Chapel Bill."

Coach Bill Belichick is widely regarded as one of the best head football coaches in the history of professional football. As the self-proclaimed "Coach Bill Belichick's number one fan", I can confirm that Coach Bill Belichick holds many coaching records, including the mind-blowing record of having won the most Super Bowl wins (six) as a head coach. Coach Bill Belichick won all of his Super Bowls while serving as the head coach of The New England Patriots. Coach Bill Belichick also won two additional Super Bowls while serving as the defensive coordinator for

9

the New York Giants during a time when they were known for having an amazing defense. Coach Bill Belichick owns the record for eight combined total Super Bowl victories as coach and coordinator. Coach Bill Belichick is known as a legendary football historian, and is referred to by many as the ultimate "student of the game." Coach Bill Belichick has a vast and ever expanding deep knowledge of the nuances of the game and the intricacies of each player's position on the football field. During Coach Bill Belichick's career with the New England Patriots, Coach Bill Belichick was the leading personality, figure, manager, and leader. He served as both the head coach and what most called the "de facto" general manager during the years of the New England Dynasty, which spanned nearly two decades from 2001 to 2019. As "Coach Bill Belichick's number one fan", it is hard for me to not cry while typing this.

1975 - Coach Bill Belichick graduated from college in 1975 from Wesleyan University, where Coach Bill Belichick played both lacrosse and football. When not investing his time becoming the best football coach in the history of professional football, Coach Bill Belichick found the time to co-create three children Amanda, Stephen and Brian with his now ex-wife, Debby Clarke Belichick.

COACH BILL BELICHICK
CAREER QUICK SUMMARY:

1975 - During the year of 1975, Coach Bill Belichick began his epic coaching career, all while working as an assistant for the Baltimore Colts. All before he ultimately became the defensive coordinator for the New York Giants in 1985 where he won two Super Bowls under the leadership of head coach, Bill Parcells. Coach Bill Belichick was named head coach of the Cleveland Browns during the year of 1991 where he led the Cleveland team for five football seasons. Coach Bill Belichick also coached with the New England Patriots and the New York Jets before becoming the head coach of The New England Patriots in 2000.

COACH BILL BELICHICK CAREER TIMELINE:

1952 - Coach Bill Belichick was birthed on Earth in Nashville, Tennessee, on April 16, 1952 as the son of Jeannette (née Munn) and Steve Belichick. Although Coach Bill Belichick went on to become God's Gift to football, contrary to popular belief I do believe no immaculate conception was involved in the creation of Coach Bill Belichick. As the self-proclaimed "Coach Bill Belichick's number one fan", I believe that all should know that Coach Bill Belichick was named after College Football Hall of Fame coach Bill Edwards, who was also Coach Bill Belichick's godfather.

Coach Bill Belichick is of Croatian ancestry, his paternal grandparents, Marija Barković and Ivan Biličić, immigrated from Draganić in 1897 and settled in Monessen, Pennsylvania. This is where they changed their names to Mary and John Belichick at the suggestion of immigration officers. Unfortunately, despite my desire to make things right, Croatia has still not yet changed their name to "Belichick" in honor of Coach Bill Belichick.

Coach Bill Belichick was raised in Annapolis, Maryland, where he was directly mentored by another legendary football coach and father, Steve Belichick. Coach Bill Belichick's father, Steve Belichick was an assistant football coach at the United States Naval Academy. Coach Bill Belichick has communicated that his father was perhaps the most important football mentor in his life. Coach Bill Belichick would consistently study football with his father, Steve Belichick. Coach Bill Belichick reportedly was taught how to break down game film at a very young age as a result of watching his father, Steve Belichick as he would diligently do his job while working as a football coach at Navy. Most Americans and American football fans do not know this, but Coach Bill Belichick's father, Steve Coach Bill Belichick wrote the most profound book in the history of football, "Football Scouting Methods," a book that Coach Bill Belichick cites as highly influential in his development as a coach.

The man who would go on to become the legendary NFL coach, Coach Bill Belichick graduated from Annapolis High School during the year 1970 where he would be a classmate of "the" Sally Brice-O'Hara. Sally Brice-O'Hara would go on to become the Vice Commandant of the Coast Guard.

While at Annapolis High School, Coach Bill Belichick played both football and lacrosse, with football being his favorite sport. Coach Bill Belichick then enrolled at Phillips Academy in Andover, Massachusetts, for a postgraduate year, with the goal of raising and improving his grades and test scores so he could be admitted to a higher quality college. Although I personally believe that The Phillips Academy might want to consider renaming themselves to be The Belichick Academy of Andover, The Phillips Academy in Andover, Massachusetts later honored Coach Bill Belichick 40 years later by inducting him into its Athletics Hall of Honor in 2011, while deciding to not rename the school as The Belichick Academy of Andover.

Coach Bill Belichick then attended Wesleyan University in Middletown, Connecticut, where he played both center and tight end. In addition to becoming a member of the football team, Coach Bill Belichick played lacrosse and a racquet-based game called squash, all while serving as the captain of the lacrosse team during his senior season. You might be asking, what is squash? Squash, which is often called squash rackets, is a racket sport played by two (singles) or four players (doubles) in a four-walled court with a small, hollow, rubber ball. The players then alternate in striking the ball with their rackets onto the playable surfaces of the four walls of the court.

Coach Bill Belichick became a member of Chi Psi fraternity en route to earning a bachelor's degree in economics in 1975. Coach Bill Belichick eventually was part of the inaugural induction class into the University's Athletics Hall of Fame in spring of 2008.

Before graduating from Wesleyan University in 1975, Coach Bill Belichick was reportedly known as nearly the exact polar opposite of his current reserved coaching and leadership persona. Coach Bill Belichick's Classmates recall that as president of the Chi Psi fraternity, the son of Navy's football scout and future NFL Hall of Famer, Coach Bill Belichick could usually be found in the vicinity of frat guys peeing on rival houses and blasting soda machines with a shotgun. Some speculate, but it cannot be proven that Coach Bill Belichick inspired Will Ferrall's "old School" character.

1975 - After graduating from Wesleyan University, Coach Bill Belichick took a $25 per week job as an assistant for the Baltimore Colts head coach Ted Marchibroda. In 1976, Coach Bill Belichick then joined the Detroit Lions as their assistant special teams coach before being asked to also add the tight ends and wide receivers coaching duties to his responsibilities list in 1977. Unfortunately, the team failed to recognize the greatness of the young Coach Bill Belichick. Coach Bill Belichick was dismissed with head coach Tommy Hudspeth and the rest of the coaching staff on January 9, 1978, a day that will forever be remembered as "The Day of Infamy". Coach Bill Belichick then invested the 1978 season working with the Denver Broncos as their assistant special teams coach and defensive assistant while also working on the team as director of films. Obsessed with football and becoming the best coach he could possibly be, Coach Bill Belichick was building himself into the ultimate National Football League coach one job at a time.

Since the time he started his legendary NFL coaching career, Coach Bill Belichick has been called several different nicknames. During Coach Bill Belichick's stints in Detroit and Denver led to the nicknames such as "Boy Genius" and "Punk." While working in New York for the New York Giants under Coach Bill Parcells, Coach Parcells called Coach Bill Belichick "Doom and Gloom" for his aloof demeanor. As "Coach Bill Belichick's number one fan" I would suggest that Coach Bill Parcells should refer to Coach Bill Belichick as "The Master," "The Wise One," "The Yoda of Coaching" and "The Best Coach In the World Ever."

1976 – The future NFL legend, Coach Bill Belichick joined the Detroit Lions as an assistant special teams coach. He was fired along with the rest of Tommy Hudspeth's coaching staff at the end of the 1977 season.

1979 – After one year with the Denver Broncos, Coach Bill Belichick began a 12-year career with the New York Giants, joining the team as a New York Giants special teams coach where he first worked as an assistant football coach under Ray Perkins. Coach Bill Belichick then helped to guide the legendary New York Giants defense while serving under the iconic football coach, Coach Bill Parcells. Together Coach Bill Parcells and Coach Bill Belichick lead the Giants to win two Super Bowls. During his time coaching the New York Giants, Coach Bill Belichick added linebacker coaching to his duties in 1980. He was named defensive coordinator in 1985 under head coach Bill Parcells, who had replaced Perkins in 1983. After expanding Coach Bill Belichick's duties, the Giants won Super Bowl XXI and Super Bowl XXV following the 1986 and 1990 seasons.

Coach Bill Belichick's legendary defensive game plan from the New York Giants' 20–19 upset victory of the Buffalo Bills in Super Bowl XXV has been placed in the Pro Football Hall of Fame, where it will stand forever as a mind-expanding coaching example for future aspiring NFL coaches. As "Coach Bill Belichick's number one fan", I would suggest you and your family consider planning a family vacation to visit the NFL Hall of Fame in Canton, Ohio so that you and your family can be educated about the legendary New York Giants' 20–19 upset victory of the Buffalo Bills in Super Bowl XXV.

1991 – At age 38, Coach Bill Belichick was hired as the head coach of the (original) Cleveland Browns making him the league's youngest head coach by six years. As the head coach of an NFL team for the first time, Coach Bill Belichick showcased his beautiful and perfectly stoic personality and commanding leadership skills that he would become known for during his time in New England. The Browns went 11-5 and reached the second round of the playoffs in 1994, however, during the 1995 season owner Art Modell announced his decision to move the NFL team to Baltimore, Maryland. The Browns, 4-5 at the time, finished 5-11 and then the Browns made one of the biggest mistakes in the history of professional football, they fired the football legend, Coach Bill Belichick. Despite having been given assurances that he would coach the new team that would later become the Baltimore Ravens, Coach Bill Belichick was instead fired on February 14, 1996, a day that will forever chill the bones of Cleveland Browns fans.

When Coach Bill Belichick cut Cleveland's popular quarterback, Bernie Kosas from their roster, Coach Bill Belichick was so hated in Cleveland, he began to receive death threats from Bernie Kosar loyalists and local broadcaster Casey Coleman received death threats as well because he unapologetically supported Coach Bill Belichick's decision. Both men got FBI protection until the death threats stopped. As "Coach Bill Belichick's number one fan", I believe that the FBI should consider renaming themselves as "For Belichick Individuals" to improve the amount of respect that they are given in the current political climate.

During Coach Bill Belichick's time as the head coach of the Cleveland Browns, coincidentally, Coach Bill Belichick's lone playoff victory was achieved against the New England Patriots, who were coached by former Giants head coach Bill Parcells, in the Wild Card Round during that postseason. During Coach Bill Belichick's final season in Cleveland, the Browns finished 5–11 despite starting 3–1. One of Coach Bill Belichick's most controversial moves was his decision to cut quarterback Bernie Kosar midway through the 1993 season. Bernie Kosar was signed by the Dallas Cowboys two days later and won a Super Bowl with the Cowboys in Super Bowl XXVIII as a backup.

In the 2013 episode of A Football Life on the Cleveland Browns relocation controversy, many sports journalists who obsessively researched and covered the Browns at the time said that in retrospective, Coach Bill Belichick actually laid the groundwork for the Ravens success in the ensuing decades. This included their win in Super Bowl XXXV (with Cleveland holdovers Matt Stover and Rob Burnett still with the team at that point), setting up the infrastructure by giving recently retired tight end Ozzie Newsome his first front-office job and had planned on drafting Ray Lewis in the 1996 NFL Draft if Belichick and the team stayed in Cleveland. If it were possible, as "Coach Bill Belichick's number one fan", I would like to credit Coach Bill Belichick as being the reason for the success of the Baltimore Ravens, the New England Patriots, the National Football League & America!

In fact, the newly-named Baltimore Ravens did draft Lewis, who went on to have a legendary 17-year Hall of Fame career with the team.

1996 SEASON - Coach Bill Belichick was reunited with his football mentor, Coach Bill Parcells, who was now the head coach in New England. The New England Patriots reached the Super Bowl that season; Coach Bill Belichick was reported to have softened personally, including cultivating a relationship with team owner Robert Kraft.

Coach Bill Belichick served under Coach Bill Parcells again as assistant head coach and defensive backs coach with the New England Patriots for the 1996 season. The Patriots finished with an 11–5 record and won the AFC Championship over the Jacksonville Jaguars, but then lost to the Green Bay Packers in Super Bowl XXXI amid rumors of Coach Bill Parcells's impending defection. Some have speculated (mostly me), that if Coach Bill Belichick would have been allowed to be the head coach during the Super

Bowl versus the Green Packers, the New England Patriots would have won. As "Coach Bill Belichick's number one fan", these are the things I think about without ceasing.

1997 SEASON – Coach Bill Parcells and Robert Kraft's relationship was not positive and it completely fell apart during the Super Bowl week, and Coach Parcells flew home separate from the team after the loss to Green Bay. Coach Bill Parcells then arrived on a deal that would allow him to take over the New York Jets. Robert Kraft refused to relinquish his rights, leaving Coach Bill Belichick as the head coach briefly. Coach Bill Parcells eventually negotiated his release, restoring Coach Bill Belichick as his top assistant and contractually stipulated heir.

NEW YORK JETS (1997–1999)

Unbeknownst to most people and most Coach Bill Belichick fans, Coach Bill Belichick had two stints as the head coach of the New York Jets without ever actually coaching an NFL game.

In February 1997, Belichick, who had been an excellent and standout assistant coach under Bill Parcells with the New York Giants and New England Patriots, was named the Jets interim head coach while the Jets and Patriots continued to negotiate compensation to release Coach Bill Parcells from his contract with the New England Patriots which would then allow Coach Bill Parcells to coach the Jets. Just six days later, the New England Patriots and the

New York Jets reached an agreement that allowed Parcells to coach the New York Jets, and Coach Bill Belichick simultaneously became the team's assistant head coach and defensive coordinator.

When Coach Bill Parcells decided to step down and no longer be the head coach of the New York Jets, after the 1999 season, he had already arranged with team management to have Coach Bill Belichick succeed him. However, Coach Bill Belichick was only the New York Jets' head football coach for just a day. On January 4, 2000, after Coach Bill Belichick was announced as the new head coach of the New York Jets, he turned his first press conference into a surprise resignation announcement. Just moments before walking up to the podium, Coach Bill Belichick wrote down a resignation note on a napkin that read, in its entirety, "I resign as HC of the NYJ." He then proceeded to deliver a half-hour speech explaining his resignation to the members of the media, that had assembled to meet the new head coach of the New York Jets.

TOM BRADY TAKES OVER AS THE QUARTERBACK FOR THE NEW ENGLAND PATRIOTS

Tom Brady remained the starter for the rest of the National Football League season and New England made a run to the Super Bowl where they actually upset St. Louis Rams' and what was called at the time, the "Greatest Show on Turf." This was the first Super Bowl win in the history of the New England Patriots' franchise.

2003 SEASON — During the 2003 season the Patriots won the Super Bowl for a second time in three seasons under Coach Bill Belichick's leadership. The Patriots won the Super Bowl that year, in a 32-29 victory over Carolina Panthers in Super Bowl 38, which was held at Reliant Stadium in Houston, Texas.

It has been reported that Coach Bill Belichick was not excited about becoming the head coach of the New York Jets, because the New York Jets appeared to be reluctantly promoting Coach Bill Belichick to become their next head coach. As stated above, after just one day on the job, Coach Bill Belichick resigned from the position and moved to become the legendary, iconic and epic New England Patriots head coach the following year. As a man who is often referred to as "Coach Bill Belichick's number one fan" I believe that the New York Jets should have considered renaming their team, The New York Coach Bill Belichick's in order to keep the coaching legend, Coach Bill Belichick as their head coach. The executives leading The New York Jets should have even considered shaving their heads and getting Coach Bill Belichick's name tattooed on top of their heads to demonstrate their appreciation and commitment to Coach Bill Belichick.

Soon after this bizarre turn of events, Belichick was introduced as the 12th full-time head coach of the New England Patriots officially succeeding Coach Pete Carroll who had recently been fired. The Patriots had inquired to the New York Jets about getting permission to interview Coach Bill Belichick for their vacant spot at head coach just prior to Coach Bill Parcells deciding to step down. Coach Bill Parcells and the New York Jets stated that Coach Bill Belichick was still under contract to the New York Jets and thus, they demanded compensation from the New England Patriots. The NFL Commissioner at the time, Paul Tagliabue agreed, and the New England Patriots gave the New York Jets a first-round draft pick in 2000 in exchange for the right to hire the future coaching legend, Coach Blll Belichick.

April 2000 — In April of 2000, the New England Patriots selected former Michigan quarterback Tom Brady 199th overall in the sixth round of the NFL draft. Coach Bill Belichick listed him on his roster as the Patriots' fourth quarterback with Tom Brady only actually appearing in one game during the entirety of his rookie season. The New England Patriots finished the season with a 5 win and 11 loss record under Coach Bill Belichick's leadership. As "Coach Bill Belichick's number one fan", I should make it known that Coach Bill Belichick himself chose not to actually play during any of the games during this season. Some have speculated that Coach Bill Belichick inserted himself into the starting lineup on both the offensive and defensive sides of the ball.

When Coach Bill Belichick arrived at The New England Patriots in 2000, the Patriots had just finished their season 8-8 under the leadership of Pete Carroll. When Coach Bill Belichick arrived in Foxborough, Massachusetts he intended to completely overhaul the roster and to build a team capable of creating the winning culture that Coach

Bill Belichick had envisioned. When Coach Bill Belichick started his reign as the head coach of the New England Patriots he had several compensatory draft picks available which were earned by Peter Carroll in 1999, when Coach Peter Carroll decided to let many veterans leave the team during the free agency period because of salary cap concerns. Thus, The Patriots had earned two compensatory sixth-round picks in the 2000 draft, which were likely as a result of the departures of defenders Mark Wheeler and Todd Collins, both of which were no longer in the NFL at the end of the 2000 season.

Demonstrating yet again his coaching genius, Coach Bill Belichick decided to use one of those compensatory sixth-round picks to draft a quarterback. The New England Patriots had debated back and forth about drafting Louisiana Tech's Tim Rattay or Michigan's Tom Brady. However, it has been reported the quarterbacks coach, Dick Rehbein, was allowed to cast the deciding vote in the draft room, and thus the team made the decision to draft Tom Brady! Tim Rattay went on to start 18 games for the San Francisco 49ers and Tom Brady eventually would become the most accomplished, celebrated and successful player in the history of The National Football League.

2001 SEASON — During the 2001 season, Coach Bill Belichick decided to promote Tom Brady to become Drew Bledsoe's backup. However, during Week 2 of the season, Coach Bill Belichick inserted Tom Brady into the game against the New York Jets because Drew Bledsoe suffered a concussion and a collapsed lung after receiving a devastating hit late in the fourth quarter of a 10-3 loss. Although Drew Bledsoe was a highly paid fan favorite, Coach Bill Belichick saw the potential of a young Tom Brady.

COACH BILL BELICHICK HAS A YODA-LEVEL INFLUENCE IN HIS COACHING LIFE

Although most Coach Bill Belichick fans do not know this, Coach Bill Belichick does have his own source to which he goes to receive sage football coaching advice. Yes! Coach Bill Belichick does in fact have his own figurate Yoda! In fact, the voice that Coach Bill Belichick is most frequently listening to while wearing those legendary headphones is none other than the voice of his long-time friend and mentor, Coach Ernie Adams. Coach Bill Belichick and Ernie Adams met in 1970 and the two have been almost inseparable since. Ernie Adams was known for years officially as The New England Patriots "Director of Football Research," but true Coach Bill Belichick fans refer to Coach Ernie Adams as the Yoda of Coach Bill Belichick. Throughout the games, Ernie Adams and his steadying strategic voice suggests plays and unique adjustments that he believes Coach Bill Belichick should be making throughout the game. Ernie Adams has vast football knowledge and an uncanny ability to make sports math calculations from the press box. Ernie Adams is a very private man and thus very few photos of Ernie Adams can be found on the internet.

2004 SEASON - During the 2004 season, the New England Patriots lead by Coach Bill Belichick, reached the status of an all-out indisputable dynasty and the ultimate team of the 2000s by winning their third Super Bowl victory in just four years, by beating the Philadelphia Eagles 24-21. Coach Bill Belichick led the New England Patriots to became the seventh franchise to win back-to-back Super Bowl titles.

COACH BILL BELICHICK AND JON BON JOVI ARE CLOSE FRIENDS

Although Coach Bill Belichick is known for his stoic personality, he does consider the high-energy rocker, Jon Bon Jovi as one of his closest friends. The two initially met and became friends when Coach Bill Belichick was coaching for the New York Giants in the early 1980's. The legendary and iconic singer even brought the very hesitant Coach Bill Belichick and Patriots defensive coordinator Charlie Weis on stage to perform a song. "That happened one time and it was unforgettable," Coach Bill Belichick once said when describing the once-in-a-life-time performance.

2006 SEASON — The New England Patriots set an NFL record with 10 consecutive postseason victories by beating the Jacksonville Jaguars 28-3. The New England Patriots milestone surpassed the nine straight playoff victories record previously set by the Green Bay Packers in the 196'0s. As a man who is considered by myself and several others as "Coach Bill Belichick's number one fan" this section of the book and the detailed documenting of

Coach Bill Belichick's success pushes me to the verge of tears. However, we must continue on as we fight back the tears.

COACH BILL BELICHICK'S SON IS A PROFESSIONAL FOOTBALL COACH

Stephen C. Belichick was born on March 25, 1987 and is an American college football coach who is the defensive coordinator for the University of Washington, a position he has held since 2024. However, Stephen Belichick is expected to rejoin his father (Coach Bill Belichick) in 2025 as Defensive Coordinator for the North Carolina football team following the 2024 New Year's Eve Sun Bowl versus Louisville. Stephen was a respected assistant coach for the New England Patriots of the National Football League (NFL) from 2012 to 2023.

2007 SEASON — This season was a difficult season for long-time die-hard committed and focused Patriots fans like myself. A New England videographer was accused of recording defensive signals by the New York Jets during the Patriots' season-opening win and that is when the now infamous "Spygate" began! An NFL investigation then validated the accusations. The New England Patriots were fined $250,000 and lost a first-round draft pick for violating the National Football League rules against using video to steal signals. Coach Bill Belichick was fined $500,000 in the incident. This situation began to sew seeds of widespread distrust of Coach Bill Belichick, the Patriots and America as a whole (in some countries). Despite leaked footage that emerged in the NFL's investigations and findings, I believe that Coach Bill Belichick is the greatest coach in the history of football and we have no proof that Bill was watching the video in question.

2008 - SEASON - The 2008 season was a glorious season for the New England Patriots. The Patriots were defending AFC champions and Coach Bill Belichick was "Belichicking" and setting records as only Coach Bill Belichick can do. Despite finishing the regular season with an incredible 11–5 record, the Patriots did not actually qualify for the playoffs. Allowing them to set another record and to become the first 11-win team since the expansion to a 12-team playoff in 1990 to miss the playoffs, as well as remarkably on the second team (after the 1985 Denver Broncos). The New England Patriots also became the first team since the 1935 Chicago Bears to go undefeated in the previous regular football season to miss the playoffs the next season.

COACH BILL BELICHICK'S SON BRIAN BELICHICK IS A PROFESSIONAL FOOTBALL COACH

Coach Brian Belichick is an American football coach and safeties coach for the New England Patriots of the National Football League (NFL). Coach Brian Belichick joined the organization as a scouting assistant in 2016, and worked as a coaching assistant from 2017 to 2019 before being promoted to safeties coach prior to the 2020 season.

2009 - The 2009 season for the New England Patriots was their 50th season overall and their 10th season under the leadership of Coach Bill Belichick. They finished the season with a solid record of 10–6, all while earning a division title before losing to the Baltimore Ravens during the NFL playoffs. It is worth mentioning that Coach Bill Belichick was not playing quarterback during the team's loss to the Baltimore Ravens.

COACH BILL BELICHICK'S DAUGHTER AMANDA BELICHICK IS A WOMEN'S LACROSSE HEAD COACH

Amanda Belichick has been a head coach at Holy Cross working as the head coach for the women's lacrosse program. Amanda is Coach Bill Belichick's eldest child and only daughter. Amanda Belichick was born in 1984 and she graduated in 2007 from Wesleyan University, where she earned a degree in history. Amanda was a lacrosse coach at her alma mater before being named the head coach of the women's lacrosse team at the College of the Holy Cross in 2015.

2010 - The 2010 season for the New England Patriots' was their 51st season as a franchise overall. Coach Bill Belichick led the Patriots where they improved on their 10–6 record from the 2009 season by finishing the year with a league-best 14–2 record which allowed them to clinch the top seed in the AFC, before losing to the New York Jets in the playoffs. It should be noted that Coach Bill Belichick was not playing quarterback during the team's loss to the New York Jets.

THE BEST COACH IN NFL HISTORY (COACH BILL BELICHICK) WAS HANDED THE LARGEST FINE IN NFL HISTORY

After the New England Patriots employee was caught videotaping defensive hand signals from the New York Jets in 2007, the National Football League decided to hit Coach Bill Belichick with a $500,000 fine, which was the largest in league history and roughly 12 percent of the $4.2 million salary he was reported to have earned that year. As the "Number One Coach Bill Belichick Fan" this situation showcased to me that Coach Bill Belichick is a polymath and a true master of football coaching, videography, lip reading, and research.

The New England Patriots chose to respond to this adverse situation by going on to average an NFL-best 36.8 points per game and beating their first eight football opponents by a mind-blowing combined 204 points!

Tom Brady went on to win the league MVP during this season after leading the National Football League with an amazing 4,806 yards passing. Tom Brady set the single-season record with 50 TD throws. The New England Patriots also completed a perfect regular season while finishing the season with a 16-0 record after they cemented their dominance by coming from behind to win an EPIC 38-35 comeback victory over the New York Giants. The New England Patriots were the first NFL team since the 1972 Dolphins to win every game on the schedule during the entire regular season. However, the team lost to the New York Giants during the Super Bowl suffering a 17-14 loss and killing their hopes of having an unbeaten season. Even simply writing about this loss feels like opening a fresh wound and pouring salt in it.

2011 SEASON - During the 2011 season, The New England Patriots finished their regular season with a solid 13-3 record and they then earned their fifth trip to The Super Bowl under the coaching genius and legendary leadership of Coach Bill Belichick. However, they were again stopped by the New York Giants when they suffered a 21-17 loss during the Super Bowl. I may or may not be continuously emotionally attempting to cope with the long-term pain and suffering associated with watching The New England Patriots suffer another Super Bowl loss.

2012 - During the 2012 season, Coach Bill Belichick carried the team to a 12-4 record with the Patriots ultimately losing to the Baltimore Ravens in the AFC Championship Game. Despite the fact that I and several other fans wanted Coach Bill Belichick to insert himself into the game as the team's starting linebacker to insure a victory over the Ravens, Coach Bill Belichick remained his humble self, and he decided to not call his own number and insert himself as the starting linebacker during the game.

2013 - Aaron Hernandez was drafted by The New England Patriots in the fourth round in 2010 and was signed to a $40 million contract extension in 2012. Before joining the Patriots, Aaron Hernandez played tight end for the Florida Gators where he caught the passes thrown by the great Tim Tebow. However, Aaron Hernandez was arrested on a murder charge of Odin Lloyd. Aaron Hernandez who had experienced tremendous success while playing college football with Tim Tebow at the University of Florida was an incredible on-the-field talent and a powerful offensive weapon for The New England Patriots, however his off the field life decisions ultimately landed him in prison after he was convicted of murder in 2015.

WHAT IS THE BELICHICK FOUNDATION?

On the website The Coach Bill Belichick Foundation states, "The Coach Bill Belichick Foundation aims to provide coaching, mentorship, and financial support to individuals, communities, and organizations focusing on football and lacrosse. Its mission is to bring the values of the Belichick family – a love of sports, coaching and team building – to the athletic leaders of tomorrow." However, I believe that the website should read, "The Coach Bill Belichick Foundation aims to improve the world by providing the world with more Coach Bill Belichick in a world that aspires to be more like Coach Bill Belichick."

Unknown to most, Coach Bill Belichick created the Coach Bill Belichick Foundation in 2013 with the goal of providing financial support to individuals, communities and organizations focused on football and lacrosse.

2014 SEASON - During the season of 2014, The New England Patriots finished their third straight regular season with 12 wins and they earned their sixth trip to the Super Bowl under the consistent and diligent leadership of the hooded one, Coach Bill Belichick. This game ended in very dramatic fashion when the undrafted rookie by the name of Malcomb Butler was able to intercept the Seattle Seahawks and their quarterback Russell Wilson's short pass into the endzone. The Patriots ended up winning this Super Bowl over the Seattle Seahawks 28-24. As a bonus note, and as "Coach Bill Belichick's number one fan", I would highly recommend that anyone suffering from depression or looking for a great way to kickstart your life should watch the NFL Films Coach Bill Belichick documentary, Do Your Job Well every morning for one-year straight or until your brain explodes.

2015 SEASON - During the 2015 season, I was the self-proclaimed "Number One Coach Bill Belichick Fan" and turned 35 years old, while New England dominated the season while earning a 12–4 record for the fourth straight season. The New England Patriots (Or The New England Belichicks as I call them) defeated the Kansas City Chiefs in a highly contested Divisional Round with a final score of 27–20. However, during the AFC Championship Game, the Patriots barely lost to the Denver Broncos who would go on to win the Super Bowl that year. The Patriots lost to the Denver Broncos by a score of 20-18. Some (mainly me) have speculated that The Patriots would have won that game if Coach Bill Belichick had put his perpetual humbleness aside and would have allowed himself to play quarterback, center, and tight end during the game.

2016 SEASON - During the 2016 season, The New England Patriots earned yet another Super Bowl win in EPIC and historic fashion as the team rallied from behind and a 28-3 deficit in the third quarter of the game to achieve a historic victory over the Atlanta Falcons 34-28 in Super Bowl 51. This game was amazing, historic, and inspiring to anyone who had a pulse and was watching, although we have no proof that dead people were not also inspired by this historic victory as well. This game marked the largest comeback victory in the history of the Super Bowl and it officially blew my mind! The Patriots joined the Pittsburgh Steelers (six), the Dallas Cowboys (five) and the San Francisco 49ers (five) as the only National Football League teams to win at least five Super Bowls! If anyone from the National Football League is reading this book I would recommend that the big game should be renamed the "Super Bill."

BEHOLD, THE POWER OF THE HOODIE

According to ESPN's Michael Wilbon, Coach Bill Belichick decided to wear a hoodie to protest the fact that the National Football League would not allow Coach Bill Belichick to wear a suit on the sidelines while coaching during NFL games. Thus, Coach Bill Belichick today can usually be found on the sideline wearing his legendary hooded sweatshirt which often looks to have been previously worn by pirates stranded on a deserted island for a solid decade.

2017 SEASON - During the year of 2017, the New England Patriots made their eighth Super Bowl appearance under the legendary Coach Bill Belichick, but they lost to the Philadelphia Eagles who used a "Philly Special" trick play to beat The New England Patriots.

COACH BILL BELICHICK DEVELOPED HIS PASSION FOR COACHING FROM HIS FATHER

Coach Bill Belichick was born as William Stephen Belichick On April 16, 1952, in Nashville Tennessee, and he was the only son of Bill and Jeannette Belichick. Coach Bill Belichick inherited his father's obsessive passion for the game of football. Coach Bill Belichick witnessed his father work as an assistant coach and a local football scout at local colleges. As Coach Bill Belichick grew up, he followed along and shadowed with his father where he often attended coaching sessions, meetings and practices.

2018 SEASON - During the year of 2018, the New England Patriots promptly rebounded from their Super Bowl loss to the Philadelphia Eagles, and they made their ninth appearance in a Super Bowl game that year! Coach Bill Belichick and Tom Brady lead the New England Patriots to throttle the Rams 13-3 and capture the coveted Lombardi Trophy once again! This Super Bowl victory allowed Coach

Bill Belichick to join George Halas and Curly Lambeau as the only coaches with six NFL championships. Just typing this brings me so much joy, it's unspeakable. Thus, I am simply typing this.

2019 MARCH - Tom Brady decided to relocate his physical body to Tampa Bay to play for the Tampa Bay Buccaneers. However, as "The Number One Coach Bill Belichick Fan" I was concerned that Tom Brady may have left his soul in New England. I believe he has since returned to New England to retrieve his soul since retiring.

2020 SEASON - Coach Bill Belichick acquired former MVP Cam Newton to replace Tom Brady. However, the Patriots finished the season with a 7-9 record. For the record, Coach Bill Belichick demonstrated even more humbleness by choosing to not call his own number to play quarterback during the 2020 season. Tom Brady then used everything he learned from Coach Bill Belichick to lead the Buccaneers to a Super Bowl win, earning Tom Brady his seventh Super Bowl ring. Some have called for Tom Brady to give his ring to Coach Bill Belichick since Tom Brady owes all to the greatness, the glory and the humbleness that is Coach Bill Belichick.

2021 SEASON - During the 2021 season, The New England Patriots draft former Alabama quarterback Mac Jones, who unseated quarterback Cam Newton as the Patriots starting quarterback during training camp. Mac Jones was selected as a member of the Pro Bowl despite being just a rookie and helped lead the New England Patriots to a 10-7 regular season record, thus earning Coach Bill Belichick his first playoff appearance since Brady relocated his physical body to Tampa Bay, Florida.

However the Patriots lost during their wild card to the Buffalo Bills in a 47-17 defeat. I believe that Coach Bill Belichick demonstrated his kindness by allowing the Buffalo Bills to win for a change.

2022 SEASON - Coach Bill Belichick decided to put longtime defensive coach Matt Patricia in charge of the New England Patriots offense. Mac Jones was unable to perform at the level he did during year one and the Patriots finished the season with a record of 8-9 finish.

2023 SEASON - During this season, Coach Bill Belichick rehired former offensive coordinator Bill O'Brien, however Mac Jones did not perform well and Mac Jones got benched with six games left in the season. The Patriots finished the season with a 4-13 record, which is the worst record in the history of Coach Bill Belichick's coaching career.

2024 - On January 11th 2024, Robert Kraft decided to shock the world and to not rename his team, The New England Belichicks. Coach Bill Belichick and Robert Kraft agreed to go their separate directions after 24 seasons together and six Super Bowl championships.

2024 - This year was a dark year for the football world, as Coach Bill Belichick was not serving as a head coach on either the professional or college level. Coach Bill Belichick agreed to appear every Monday afternoon during the 2024

NFL season with ESPN's The Pat McAfee Show. Coach Bill Belichick first appeared as an analyst on the show during its "5th Annual Draft Spectacular" where he covered the 2024 NFL draft.

NFL great and legendary quarterback, Peyton Manning commented about Coach Bill Belichick's draft coverage, "I can't tell you the advantage to having a defensive coach to take the quarterback behind the ropes on that defense, it made me a better quarterback, so Bill's gonna do that. I think the audience is going to be fascinated at how smart he is. Look, you guys saw how witty he is. I watched the Draft show you guys did; it was awesome. He's quick-witted, he's funny and like I said, he's brilliant when it comes to defense and offense, the guy can flat-out coach."

2024 - May - Peyton Manning shared with the world during the EPIC Netflix special The Roast of Tom Brady that Coach Bill Belichick would join another ESPN program, joining the Manning brothers (Peyton and Eli) in the Manningcast, which is an alternate live television broadcast of Monday Night Football.

2024 - NORTH CAROLINA TAR HEELS (2025–PRESENT)

On the glorious day of December 11, 2024, Coach Bill Belichick was named the 35th head football coach of the North Carolina Tar Heels football team. As the head coach of the North Carolina Tar Heels football team, this will be Coach Bill Belichick's first time coaching football on the college football level. Coach Bill Belichick will reportedly earn $10,000,000 per year, with the first three years of his contract being guaranteed. Coach Bill Belichick will also have the opportunity to earn $3.5 million per year in annual incentives. As "Coach Bill Belichick's number one fan", I would recommend that the University of Carolina should rename their college the University of North Carolina at "Chapel Bill."

Coach Bill Belichick Has Already Been Celebrated As "Chapel Bill" At North Carolina By the Local Fan Base.

102 COACH BILL BELICHICK FACTS:

STAY IN THE PLAYER'S BOX | LOOK LIKE A MILITARY OPERATION NOT A BUS STOP

https://www.nbcsports.com/boston/patriots/bill-belichick-gets-300-wins-because-his-teams-took-care-million-details

Coach Belichick is fastidious about details and making sure that his teams do the little things right. Belichick wants to instill a culture of accountability and dependability that extends into every aspect of the team. The Belichick "Do Your Job" culture then manifests and showcases itself in the form of winning on the field. Coach Bill Belichick is obsessed with making sure that his team stands within the "players box" during games.

COACH BILL BELICHICK FACT #2

THE PATRIOT WAY | PUNCH THE BALL OUT AND FORCE FUMBLES

https://www.nbcsports.com/boston/patriots/bill-belichick-gets-300-wins-because-his-teams-took-care-million-details

Coach Belichick is obsessive about details and making sure that his teams do the little things right. Unlike many coaches, Coach Bill Belichick relentlessly teaches and drills his players during practice on how to punch the ball out of the ball carrier's hands during practice.

COACH BILL BELICHICK FUN FACT #3

THE PATRIOT WAY | THE PENALTY FREE MINDSET

https://www.nbcsports.com/boston/patriots/bill-belichick-gets-300-wins-because-his-teams-took-care-million-details

Coach Bill Belichick is focused on making sure his teams do not beat themselves as a result of receiving penalties caused by mental errors and poor execution.

"It's not all about talent. It's about dependability, consistency, and being able to improve. If you work hard and you're coachable, and you understand what you need to do, you can improve."

- COACH BILL BELICHICK

COACH BILL BELICHICK FUN FACT #4

THE PATRIOT WAY |
LEARNING HOW NOT TO LOSE

https://www.nbcsports.com/boston/patriots/bill-belichick-gets-300-wins-because-his-tea

"A lot of performance is based on confidence, knowing what you're doing, and being familiar, and not thinking too much and trying to play at confident game speed."

- COACH BILL BELICHICK

Coach Bill Belichick likes to practice and drill his team until they cannot get it wrong, not until they can get it right.

COACH BILL BELICHICK FUN FACT #5

THE PATRIOT WAY |
THE LITTLE THINGS MATTER MOST

https://www.nbcsports.com/boston/patriots/bill-belichick-gets-300-wins-because-his-teams-took-care-million-details

"If you're well-prepared, you know what you're doing, and you have an idea what the opponents can do - what their strengths and weaknesses are - once you get into the game, those adjustments will be - I won't say easy, but relatively easier and more manageable."

- COACH BILL BELICHICK

COACH BILL BELICHICK FUN FACT #6

THE PATRIOT WAY | ORGANIZATION
CHANGES THE CONVERSATION WHICH
LEADS TO DOMINATION

https://www.nbcsports.com/boston/patriots/bill-belichick-gets-300-wins-because-his-teams-took-care-million-details

"What we can control is our performance and our execution, and that's what we're going to focus on."
- COACH BILL BELICHICK

COACH BILL BELICHICK FUN FACT #7

THE PATRIOT WAY |
THE PAYOFF IS THE PLAYOFFS

https://www.nbcsports.com/boston/patriots/bill-belichick-gets-300-wins-because-his-teams-took-care-million-details

Football is Coach Bill Belichick's hobby, passion, and career, and winning Super Bowls is what Coach Bill Belichick does, thus it should not be surprising to anyone that Coach Bill Belichick weaves football into his off-the-field hobbies.

Coach Bill Belichick loves boats and boating and thus Coach Bill Belichick has decided to name his boat after the number of Super Bowl rings he has earned, for Coach Bill Belichick is focused only on winning championships.

"There is an old saying about the strength of the wolf is the pack, and I think there is a lot of truth to that. On a football team, it's not the strength of the individual players, but it is the strength of the unit and how they all function together."

- COACH BILL BELICHICK

COACH BILL BELICHICK FUN FACT #8

THE PATRIOT WAY | CONSISTENCY IS KING

https://www.nbcsports.com/boston/patriots/bill-belichick-gets-300-wins-because-his-teams-took-care-million-details

> "My personal coaching philosophy, my mentality, has always been to make things as difficult as possible for players in practice, however bad we can make them, I make them."
>
> - COACH BILL BELICHICK

COACH BILL BELICHICK FUN FACT #9

THE PATRIOT WAY | DELEGATE TO DILIGENT DOERS

https://www.nbcsports.com/boston/patriots/bill-belichick-gets-300-wins-because-his-teams-took-care-million-details

> "Every single player matters. Every single player can change the course of the game."
>
> - COACH BILL BELICHICK

COACH BILL BELICHICK FUN FACT #10

THE PATRIOT WAY |
HE WAS A WILD MAN IN COLLEGE

http://mentalfloss.com/article/91747/11-things-you-might-not-know-about-bill-belichick

Before Coach Bill Belichick graduated from Wesleyan University in 1975, he was reportedly nearly the reverse of how most observers would describe as his current stoic and focused personality. Classmates who attended college with Coach Bill Belichick recall that as the president of the Chi Psi fraternity, Coach Bill Belichick could often be found during college near the area and location of the frat guys that were urinating on the rival houses when not shooting vending machines with a shotgun.

https://archive.boston.com/sports/football/patriots/articles/2012/02/05/friends_know_a_different_bill_belichick_than_patriots_fans_do/?page=3

COACH BILL BELICHICK FUN FACT #11

THE PATRIOT WAY | HE WAS ONCE PUBLIC ENEMY #1 IN CLEVELAND

http://mentalfloss.com/article/91747/11-things-you-might-not-know-about-bill-belichick

Before Coach Bill Belichick decided to leave The Browns and to join the New England Patriots, Coach Bill Belichick invested four years as the head coach of the Cleveland Browns. When Coach Bill Belichick felt it was time to cut Cleveland's popular and fan favorite quarterback, Bernie Kosar, he began to receive death threats. A local sports broadcaster by the name of Casey Coleman who showed support for Coach Bill Belichick's decision to cut Bernie Kosar also received threats. Ultimately, both men had to secure protection from the FBI until the death threats stopped.

COACH BILL BELICHICK FUN FACT #12

THE PATRIOT WAY |
THE MAN, THE MYTH, THE NICKNAMES

http://mentalfloss.com/article/91747/11-things-you-might-not-know-about-bill-belichick

During Coach Bill Belichick's coaching career and en route to becoming the most successful NFL coach of all-time, Coach Bill Belichick was known as "Boy Genius" and "Punk" while serving as an assistant coach for the Detroit Lions and the Denver Broncos. While working as an assistant coach for Coach Bill Parcells in New York, Coach Bill Belichick was referred to as "Doom and Gloom" by Coach Bill Parcells because of Coach Bill Belichick's stoic, focused and determined demeanor.

As the "Number One Coach Bill Belichick" fan I would suggest the following nicknames for Coach Bill Belichick:

» "Chapel Bill"   » "The Greatest of All Time"
» "The Legend"   » "The Hooded Goat"
» "The Great One"

COACH BILL BELICHICK FUN FACT #13

THE PATRIOT WAY | BILL HAS FORKED OVER BIG MONEY IN FINES FROM THE NFL

http://mentalfloss.com/article/91747/11-things-you-might-not-know-about-bill-belichick

After a New England Patriots employee was caught videotaping the defensive hand signals from the New York Jets during the 2007 season, the National Football League hit Coach Bill Belichick with a $500,000 fine, which was the largest fine in the history of the National Football League and roughly 12% of the reported $4.2 million salary he was supposed to earn that year. It should be noted that it was never proven that Coach Bill Belichick watched the footage that was gathered of the opposing coaches. It has also never been proven that Coach Bill Belichick had anything to do with his rouge employees deciding to film the opposing coaches.

COACH BILL BELICHICK FUN FACT #14

THE PATRIOT WAY | OUTWORK EVERYBODY REGARDLESS OF HOW MUCH YOU GET PAID

https://www.cnbc.com/2019/01/31/bill-belichick-got-his-first-nfl-job-at-23-it-paid-25-dollars-a-week.html

> "I think Tom Brady is one of the most consistent players that I've ever coached. He works hard every week. There are no ups and downs with him."
>
> - COACH BILL BELICHICK

During 1975, the 23 year old Coach Bill Belichick graduated from Wesleyan University with a goal and a vision to become a professional football coach. Because of his work ethic, Coach Bill Belichick was able to have a college coach put in a good word to Ted Marchibroda, who was the head coach of the Baltimore Colts during this time.

When Coach Bill Belichick got hired by the Baltimore Colts, he was asked to analyze game film, drive the coaches around and work the Xerox machine. Coach Belichick has described this time in his life in the following way.

"I got three meals, a bed, and a lot of football...and that was all I really wanted at the time."

At the age of 23, Coach Bill Belichick impressed his bosses and after working for free for just a couple of weeks, the Colts general manager offered to pay Coach Bill Belichick $25 per week, or $21.22 after taxes. Although at the time, the 23 year old Coach Bill Belichick didn't have an official title he had an opportunity to work for a professional football team coaching football so that he could obsessively learn the game of football all while improving his coaching skills and demonstrating his relentless work ethic.

https://www.cnbc.com/2019/01/31/bill-belichick-got-his-first-nfl-job-at-23-it-paid-25-dollars-a-week.html

COACH BILL BELICHICK FUN FACT #15

THE PATRIOT WAY |
BILL DOES NOT WANT YOUR FREE CARS

http://mentalfloss.com/article/91747/11-things-you-might-not-know-about-bill-belichick

Coach Bill Belichick Will Not Accept Cars As Gifts.

While many high-profile sports personalities receive the gift of a new car from various organizations seeking to woo and wow sports personalities, Coach Bill Belichick will have none of it. Coach Bill Belichick has often been approached by car dealerships with lucrative offers to drive their vehicles for free in hopes that he will use his celebrity status to endorse their dealership and to ultimately help them to sell more cars, but Coach Bill Belichick always says no. Coach Bill Bellichik will only buy his family cars from Farrell Volvo in Southborough, Massachusetts, a dealership owned by his long-time and life-long college friend, Jim Farrell.

COACH BILL BELICHICK FUN FACT #16

THE PATRIOT WAY |
DOING TIME TO HELP STOP CRIME

http://mentalfloss.com/article/91747/11-things-you-might-not-know-about-bill-belichick

Coach Bill Belichick generously uses his off-season time to do humanitarian work throughout the great United States of America and he is specifically interested in helping, mentoring and rehabilitating the incarcerated populations. Coach Belichick has diligently worked with former NFL legend and Hall of Fame player Jim Brown on the Amer-I-Can program, which provides both aid and support to people that are in prison. This program also invests time in visiting gang members to mentor them and attempt to prevent violence.

COACH BILL BELICHICK FUN FACT #17

THE PATRIOT WAY | TOO BUSY WINNING
GAMES TO BE IN VIDEO GAMES -

http://mentalfloss.com/article/91747/11-things-you-might-not-know-about-bill-belichick

Video game enthusiasts and long-time fans of the long-running Madden NFL video game series have often asked why they cannot find Coach Bill Belichick within the video game. Gamers often ask, why can't they ever find the legendary Coach Bill Belichick and why is there always an anonymous character by the name of Josh Moore coaching in the place of Coach Bill Belichick? Sometimes, the game will even refer to a more obscure and generic character by the name of "NE Coach." The reason is because Coach Bill Belichick refuses to join the National Football League Coaches Association which is the organization that works with Electronic Arts to license the images and likenesses of NFL coaches for the game.

COACH BILL BELICHICK FUN FACT #18

THE PATRIOT WAY |
BILL DOESN'T WASTE TIME
WITH UNNECESSARY TECHNOLOGY

http://mentalfloss.com/article/91747/11-things-you-might-not-know-about-bill-belichick

Coach Bill Belichick is known as a man who obsessively watches game film. In fact, Coach Bill Belichick first began watching game film with his father, Coach Steve Belichick in the 1950s. Coach Bill Belichick is also a man who loves and values consistency and he is also known as a man who is not fond of abandoning something that has been proven to work in favor of something that could potentially work. After attempting to use various tablets to arrange football plays and to break down other data on the sideline, Coach Bill Belichick was seen on the sidelines of a game smashing his tablet during October of 2016. Coach Bill Belichick clarified to the media about his interaction with his tablet, "As you probably noticed, I'm done with the tablets," he told the media. "They're just too undependable for me. I'm going to stick with pictures, which several of our other coaches do, as well, because there just isn't enough consistency in the performance of the tablets. I just can't take it anymore."

COACH BILL BELICHICK FUN FACT #19

THE PATRIOT WAY | OVER THE AGE OF 70 YEARS OLD, BILL WILL STILL OUTWORK YOU

Coach Bill Belichick is legendary for quotes he often says such as: "No days off."

"Do Your Job!" means being prepared, working hard, paying attention to the details and putting the team first."

- COACH BILL BELICHICK

> "I think practice preparation is always an indicator of game performance — not necessarily 100%, because there are still a lot of variables there, but it's still an indicator."
>
> - COACH BILL BELICHICK

https://www.mentalfloss.com/article/91747/11-things-you-might-not-know-about-bill-belichick

COACH BILL BELICHICK FUN FACT #20

THE PATRIOT WAY |
FOOTBALL IS IN BILL'S BLOOD

Coach Bill Belichick's father, Steve Belichick, was an assistant collegiate football coach, primarily at the United States Naval Academy, and taught his son the finer points of the sport from an early age.

https://apnews.com/5cf9bac5d3004bc387f1f51b25491797

COACH BILL BELICHICK FUN FACT #21

THE PATRIOT WAY |
HE HAS THE MOST SUPER BOWL WINS

Coach Bill Belichick stands alone with six Super Bowl wins.

Coach Bill Belichick has led six Patriots teams to Super Bowl titles, the most won by any coach in history. Former Pittsburgh Steelers coach Chuck Noll is next with four.

https://apnews.com/5cf9bac5d3004bc387f1f51b25491797

COACH BILL BELICHICK FUN FACT #22

THE PATRIOT WAY | HE COULD NOT PLAY
WELL, BUT HE CAN COACH

Although his mind was made for football, he was a limited football player who received no interest from top-division colleges and instead, played center and tight end at the smaller Wesleyan University, in Middletown, Connecticut.

https://www.britannica.com/biography/Bill-Belichick

THE PATRIOT WAY | BILL WAS AN ASSISTANT COACH FOR FIVE TEAMS

He moved on to assistant-coaching positions with the Detroit Lions and the Denver Broncos before joining the coaching staff of the New York Giants in 1979. After being fired as the head coach for the browns he took the assistant Coach position for the Patriots and Jets with Parcells.

THE PATRIOT WAY | ONE SMALL STEP FOR THE GIANTS; ONE GIANT LEAP FOR BILL-KIND.

He served as a special-teams coach and then linebackers coach before being promoted to defensive coordinator by head coach Bill Parcells in 1985. Coach Bill Parcells and Coach Bill Belichick would eventually win two Super Bowls for the New York Giants in 1987 and in 1991 with both of them coaching.

https://www.britannica.com/biography/Bill-Belichick

THE PATRIOT WAY | COACH BILL BELICHICK HAD THE OPPORTUNITY TO COACH UNDER THE HEAD COACH BILL PARCELLS

Coach Bill Belichick earned alot working as an assistant coach under the Giants, Jets, and Patriots.

https://www.britannica.com/biography/Bill-Parcells

THE PATRIOT WAY | BILL WAS ABLE TO CREATE ONE OF THE STRONGEST DEFENSES IN THE 1980S WHILE COACHING THE NEW YORK GIANTS

https://www.britannica.com/biography/Bill-Belichick

Coach Bill Belichick developed one of the NFL's most effective, dominant and will-imposing defenses during the 1980s while coaching for The New York Giants under head coach Bill Parcells. In four of Coach Bill Belichick's six seasons working as a defensive coordinator, his Giants defenses were ranked in the top five of the National Football League in terms of yards and points which were critical to the team's two Super Bowl victories (1987, 1991) that they won during this span of time. As a direct result of this ability to put together an incredible defense, he was named as the head coach of the Cleveland Browns during the year, 1991.

COACH BILL BELICHICK FUN FACT #27

THE PATRIOT WAY | BILL'S FIRST HEAD COACHING POSITION WAS FOR THE CLEVELAND BROWNS

https://www.fox61.com/article/sports/nfl/key-moments-highlights-bill-belichick-coaching-career-nfl-football/520-d17ece9e-e91c-4b7a-9c47-ec95b0bcc05d

COACH BILL BELICHICK FUN FACT #28

THE PATRIOT WAY | BILL WAS A PROUD MEMBER OF THE NEW YORK JETS FOR ONE DAY

https://www.britannica.com/biography/Bill-Belichick

COACH BILL BELICHICK FUN FACT #29

THE PATRIOT WAY | AFTER LEAVING THE JETS, BILL JOINED THE PATRIOTS

After leaving the Jets as head coach for a day he took the head coaching position at the Patriots less than a month later.

https://www.britannica.com/biography/Bill-Belichick

COACH BILL BELICHICK FUN FACT #30

THE PATRIOT WAY | ALTHOUGH COACH BILL BELICHICK WAS 5-11 DURING HIS FIRST YEAR AS THE HEAD COACH OF THE PATRIOTS, HE WAS OBSESSED WITH CREATING A CULTURE OF WINNING KNOWN AS "THE PATRIOT WAY"

https://www.britannica.com/biography/Bill-Belichick

"There are no shortcuts to building a team each season. You build the foundation brick by brick."

- COACH BILL BELICHICK

COACH BILL BELICHICK FUN FACT #31

THE PATRIOT WAY | SINCE PROMOTING TOM BRADY TO STARTING QUARTERBACK, THE TEAM HAS NEVER HAD A LOSING SEASON

https://www.britannica.com/biography/Bill-Belichick

COACH BILL BELICHICK FUN FACT #32

THE PATRIOT WAY | THE ONLY COACH WHO IS NOT A MEMBER OF THE NATIONAL FOOTBALL LEAGUE COACH'S ASSOCIATION

https://www.cbssports.com/nfl/news/why-bill-belichick-and-some-players-are-not-depicted-in-madden-nfl-or-other-video-games/

Coach Bill Belichick refuses to join the National Football League Coaches Association which is the organization that works with Electronic Arts to license the images and likenesses of NFL coaches for the game, which is why his image and likeness are never featured in The Madden video games.

COACH BILL BELICHICK FUN FACT #33

THE PATRIOT WAY | FINDING AND DEVELOPING PLAYERS THAT NOBODY ELSE WANTED

2004: CB RANDALL GAY

After a strong collegiate career at LSU, Gay went undrafted in the 2004 NFL Draft. The Patriots scooped him up and he immediately had an impact on the team's secondary, emerging as a starter while recording 34 tackles, 2 interceptions, and 6 passes defensed for the squad. He led the team in tackles during their Super Bowl 39 victory with 11. He played four seasons with the Patriots as a nickel back during the middle of his tenure and was solid, even though the team had multiple injuries to key players during that time.

2009: QB BRIAN HOYER

Hoyer emerged as the Patriots' top backup quarterback during his rookie preseason, beating out former third-round pick Kevin O'Connell, veteran Kevin Walter, and Matt Gutierrez for the job. He spent three years with the Patriots before bouncing around the league as a spot starter, logging a 16-21 record with 48 passing touchdowns and 30 interceptions. He returned to the Patriots as a backup quarterback as part of the Jimmy Garoppolo trade in 2017.

2012: RB BRANDON BOLDEN,

Bolden quickly emerged as a special teams contributor for the Patriots while averaging 4.2 yards per carry and 7.9 yards per reception during his six years with the team. He had a brief, one-year stop in Miami but returned to the team during the 2019 offseason.

2014: CB MALCOLM BUTLER

Butler is the best undrafted free agent on this list. He first made waves with his game-clinching interception of Russell Wilson in Super Bowl 49 in which he jumped Ricardo Lockette's run in the slot on the goal line. From there, he developed into the Patriots' top cornerback. Over the next three years, Butler started 47 games, intercepted eight passes, created four fumbles, broke up 44 passes, and logged 159 tackles. His final moment with the Patriots — playing just one snap in the team's Super Bowl 52 loss to the Philadelphia Eagles — was certainly confounding, but he has continued to be a strong NFL cornerback since joining the Tennessee Titans in the 2018 offseason.

2015: C DAVID ANDREWS

Andrews quickly became the Patriots' starter at center after signing with the Patriots out of Georgia. He started and was a big asset for Tom Brady in pass protection while making line calls.

2016: DB JONATHAN JONES

After a very strong career at Auburn, Jones went undrafted in the 2016 draft and signed with the Patriots. He performed well enough in the preseason to earn a job and was a key role player for the team in recent seasons. He played in every game since 2016 and logged a career-high three interceptions, 1.5 sacks, and 56 tackles in 2018.

2017: TE JACOB HOLLISTER

Hollister appeared in 15 games as a rookie for the Patriots, but he only played in 7.5 percent of the offensive snaps. He had more of an impact on special teams. He was traded to the Seattle Seahawks during the 2019 offseason.

2018: CB J.C. JACKSON

Jackson had a terrific preseason with the Patriots and earned a spot on the 53-man roster as their lone undrafted free agent in 2018. He was a key part of the Patriots' secondary rotation during his rookie season and showed off nice ball skills, grabbing three interceptions and six pass defenses in 13 games (five starts). He has the tools needed to be a quality starter and his performance was part of the reason that the team felt comfortable moving on from 2018 second-round pick Duke Dawson just ahead of 2019 roster cuts.

2019: WR GUNNER OLSZEWSKI, WR JAKOBI MEYERS

Perhaps one of the most unlikely success stories of this list is Olszewski who went undrafted out of Division II Bemidji State and got a call from the Patriots for a workout while he was digging a ditch. The Patriots converted him to wide receiver and he showed enough as a return man to make the roster despite being told earlier that he would be waived. The Patriots didn't want to risk losing him on waivers, so they decided to trade DB Keion Crossen to open up a roster spot for Olszewski.

Meanwhile, Meyers, had an excellent preseason for the Patriots and emerged quickly as a potential contributor. He caught 20 passes for 253 yards and two scores in the preseason and while he'll likely be a depth player to start his career, he showed a lot of future upside.

https://www.britannica.com/biography/Bill-Belichick

THE PATRIOT WAY | FIRST COACH TO GO UNDEFEATED IN A 16 GAME REGULAR SEASON

https://www.britannica.com/biography/Bill-Belichick

During this amazing season, Tom Brady won the league MVP leading the National Football League with a blind-blowing 4,806 yards of passing. Tom Brady set an NFL single-season record with 50 touchdown passes! The New England Patriots also completed their regular season while finishing the season with a 16-0 record. The New England Patriots were the first NFL team since the 1972 Dolphins to win every game on the schedule during the entire regular season. However, the team lost to the New York Giants during the Super Bowl suffering a 17-14 loss and killing their hopes of having an unbeaten season. As "Coach Bill Belichick's number one fan" I believe it is important for everyone to know that Coach Bill Belichick was not actually playing quarterback during his team's 17-14 loss.

THE PATRIOT WAY | COACH BILL BELICHICK LEAD THE BIGGEST COMEBACK IN SUPERBOWL HISTORY

https://www.britannica.com/biography/Bill-Belichick

In 2016 the team went an NFL-best 14–2 and cruised through the AFC playoffs en route to another Super Bowl berth. There the Patriots engineered the largest comeback in Super Bowl history, overcoming a 25-point third-quarter deficit to the Atlanta Falcons in overtime to win a fifth title, giving Belichick the most Super Bowl championships for an NFL head coach.

COACH BILL BELICHICK FACT #36

THE PATRIOT WAY | A DECADE OF DIVISION TITLE DOMINATION

https://www.britannica.com/biography/Bill-Belichick

Coach Bill Belichick is considered by most as "the greatest professional football coach" in the history of American professional football. During the 24 seasons Coach Bill Belichick was with the New England Patriots of the National Football League (NFL), he led his New England Patriots team to six Super Bowl titles (2002, 2004, 2005, 2015, 2017, and 2019), the most for an NFL head coach.

COACH BILL BELICHICK FACT #37

THE PATRIOT WAY | WON THE LOWEST SCORING SUPER BOWL GAME IN HISTORY

In what was the lowest-scoring game in Super Bowl history, the Patriots defeated the Los Angeles Rams, 13–3, and Belichick claimed his sixth title in 2018.

https://www.britannica.com/biography/Bill-Belichick

COACH BILL BELICHICK FUN FACT #38

THE PATRIOT WAY | STEPHEN BELICHICK WAS THE SAFETIES COACH FOR THE NEW ENGLAND PATRIOTS

https://images.app.goo.gl/MjWVYWTx7T1H6yTB6

Stephen C. Belichick (born March 25, 1987) is the son of Coach Bill Belichick. Stephen Belichick was a college football coach and defensive coordinator for the University of Washington, a position he held during 2024. Stephen Belichick is expected to join his father in 2025 as the official Defensive Coordinator for the North Carolina Tarheels.

Stephen Belichick was an assistant coach for the New England Patriots of the National Football League (NFL) from 2012 to 2023 while working under his father, Coach Bill Belichick.

Stephen Belichick played lacrosse at The Rivers School in Weston, Massachusetts, where he excelled and was an All-League Honorable Mention selection in his senior year. Stephen Belichick attended Rutgers University where he continued to play lacrosse as a defenseman and long-stick midfielder (LSM) from 2008 through 2011. Stephen Belichick also played for Rutgers Football team under coach Greg Schiano in 2011 as a long snapper.

COACH BILL BELICHICK FUN FACT #39

THE PATRIOT WAY | HE TRIMS DOWN THE FAT TO AVOID INFORMATION OVERLOAD

https://www.nbcsports.com/boston/patriots/tom-brady-bill-belichicks-greatness-he-trims-fat-avoid-information-overload

"Coach comes in and says, 'These are the things we need to do to win,' and he's right damn near 100 percent of the time," Brady told ESPN in 2011. "It's, 'This is what we need to do, and this is how you're going to do it, and if we don't do it, we're going to lose.'

"I would always say, sometimes coaches give you so much information that you can't retain any of it because it's so much," he said. "I think what he does is he trims the fat. He gets you the meat of what they're trying to do. He doesn't confuse you. He doesn't tell you things that may never come up. It's not information overload." - Tom Brady (The legendary New England Patriots quarterback during the reign of Coach Bill Belichick's dominance)

https://www.nbcsportsboston.com/nfl/new-england-patriots/tom-brady-on-bill-belichicks-greatness-he-trims-the-fat-to-avoid-information-overload/393724/

Coach Belichick has a fundamental belief and that is known as a "less-is-more" teaching style. Whether Coach Bill Belichick is making halftime adjustments or meeting with his entire football team to instruct his players what they need to do during a given week, his bullet points for winning in the upcoming game have now become legendary in the National Football League.

COACH BILL BELICHICK FUN FACT #40

THE PATRIOT WAY | BILL CHOOSES THE PLAYERS, BALANCES THE BUDGET AND COACHES THE TEAM

https://musketfire.com/2019/10/27/patriots-bill-belichick-head-coach-gm/

Bill earned a college degree in economics upon his graduation at Wesleyan University in 1975. Coach Bill Belichick is one of the rare NFL power figures who does double-duty as both his team's head coach and its general manager.

https://www.sunsigns.org/famousbirthdays/d/profile/bill-belichick

COACH BILL BELICHICK FUN FACT #41

THE PATRIOT WAY | NAMED COACH OF THE YEAR THREE TIMES, BUT HE IS REALLY COACH OF THE YEAR EVERY YEAR

https://www.sunsigns.org/famousbirthdays/d/profile/bill-belichick/

He has also been awarded as "Coach of the Year" thrice: in 2003, 2007 and 2010. While essentially having two full time jobs as a head coach and a general manager for the New England Patriots, it could be argued that he should be coach of the year every year.

THE PATRIOT WAY | COACH BILL BELICHICK HAS APPEARED IN OVER 20% OF THE SUPER BOWLS PLAYED DURING HIS NFL HEAD COACHING CAREER

https://247sports.com/nfl/new-england-patriots/Article/Patriots-Super-Bowl-Bill-Belichick-has-appeared-in-over-20-percent-of-Super-Bowls-114455113/

Super Bowl 52 will be played on Sunday, and as the game is Belichick's 11th, he will have appeared as a coach in 21.2 percent of the total Super Bowls according to the NFL's research team. If you cut the timeline down to when he was promoted to coordinator for the Giants, that percentage jumps to 34.3. Since Belichick became a coordinator, he has appeared in over one third of the total Super Bowls.

THE PATRIOT WAY | COACH BILL BELICHICK IS AN INCREDIBLE TALENT SCOUT

https://www.espn.com/nfl/news/story?id=3018338

THE PATRIOT WAY | COACH BILL BELICHICK'S 10 BEST MOVES AS A COACH AND GENERAL MANAGER

https://bellyupsports.com/2019/02/bill-belichicks-10-best-moves-as-a-coach-and-gm/

Move #1 – Resigning from the Jets the day after becoming their head coach, to join the Patriots. He now has a career record of 29-11 against the Jets as the Patriots Head Coach / G.M.

Move #2 – Trading a 6th round draft pick for Kyle Van Noy and a 7th round pick. Van Noy was a former 2nd round draft pick by the Lions, but didn't quite pan out the way they had hoped. Since the trade, he's become one of the Patriots best defensive players, and it showed in the 2019 post season.

Move #3 – Signing Darrelle Revis to what turned out to be a 1 year contract for 12 million dollars with a 2nd year option for an additional $20 million. Although the option didn't get picked up after his 1 year stint with New England, Revis was a big part in helping the Patriots get to and win the Super Bowl.

Move #4 – Signing Stephon Gilmore to a 5 year $65 million contract. At the time, many thought it was a strange deal, and one that the Patriots usually wouldn't hand out to a player. However, Gilmore earned every penny from that contract, coming up big for the Patriots.

Move #5 – Trading a 2nd and 7th round draft pick for Wes Welker. In his 6th season with the Patriots, Welker caught 672 passes, was a first down machine, and helped redefine the slot receiver role for the New England Patriots.

Move #6 – Drafting former Kent State quarterback Julian Edelman in the 7th round (pick 232). Belichick told Edelman after selecting him in the 2009 NFL draft: "We don't know what position you're going to play, but we know you can play ball." Edelman worked extremely hard to become a receiver in the NFL. His hard work has paid off and he won his 3rd Super Bowl and 1st Super Bowl MVP, catching 10 passes for 141 yards in the Patriots Super Bowl 53 win against the Rams.

Move #7 – Trading a 4th round draft pick to the Raiders for Randy Moss. Many thought Moss' career was over and that he was washed up, but many were wrong! Moss had his best season statistically in his first year with the Patriots in 2007, catching a record 23 touchdowns and helping the Patriots get to a 16-0 season. The Patriots ultimately came up short against the Giants in the Super Bowl, missing out on a perfect season.

Move #8 – Drafting Tom Brady in the 2000 NFL Draft in the 6th round with pick 199. There were 6 other quarterbacks selected before Brady.

Move #9 – Trusting Tom Brady to be the franchise quarterback and trading Drew Bledsoe to the division rival Buffalo Bills. Bledsoe was the Patriots' starting QB for his 8th season and was entering his 9th season as the starter before taking a scary hit that almost ended his career. The Bills traded a 1st round draft pick to their division rival for a QB entering his 10th season and Bledsoe only lasted 3 seasons in Buffalo.

Move #10 – Drafting Wisconsin running back James White from Wisconsin during the fourth round of the NFL draft. His receiving statistics exceeded his rushing statistics. He is one of two holders (the other being Darren Sproles) of the all-time record for receptions in a single playoff game, 15, which he made in the AFC divisional round playoff game following the 2018 season.

COACH BILL BELICHICK FUN FACT #45

THE PATRIOT WAY | CUTTING OFF THE SLEEVES

Coach Bill Belichick is known for cutting off the sleeves of his legendary hoodies to complete the look and style I refer to as "The Belichick".

https://espnsiouxfalls.com/i-figured-out-why-bill-belichick-wears-a-hoodie/

COACH BILL BELICHICK FUN FACT #46

THE PATRIOT WAY |
10 YEARS IN THE COACHING DESERT

Coach Bill Belichick spent 10 years in minor coaching positions in the NFL with the Baltimore Colts, Detroit Lions, Denver Broncos, and New York Giants before landing the defensive coordinator job with the Giants in 1985.

https://www.biography.com/athletes/a91277838/bill-belichick

Coach Bill Belichick built his reputation day-by-day as being the most diligent, disciplined, focused, and stoic student and teacher of the game.

COACH BILL BELICHICK FUN FACT #47

THE PATRIOT WAY | BILL HATES
INCONSISTENT TABLET TECHNOLOGY

https://www.sportsretriever.com/football/19-interesting-facts-bill-belichick-never-knew/

COACH BILL BELICHICK FUN FACT #48

THE PATRIOT WAY | MOST FORMER
MEMBERS OF HIS COACHING STAFF DO NOT
DO WELL AS HEAD COACHES

Although many members of Coach Bill Belichick's coaching staff have attempted to leave and become successful coaches on their own, it has not worked out for most of them. Most don't understand Coach Bill Belichick and his dedication to being the general manager and the head coach is what produces the winning results.

https://www.usatoday.com/story/sports/nfl/2024/01/11/bill-belichick-coaching-tree-new-england-patriots/72194740007/

COACH BILL BELICHICK FUN FACT #49

THE PATRIOT WAY | BILL LOVES PLAYING MIND GAMES WITH HIS OPPONENTS

Coach Bill Belichick is known for truly understanding the rules and nuances of the game to the point that he can get into the head of opposing coaches.

https://jetswire.usatoday.com/2017/12/31/patriots-bill-belichick-playing-some-seriously-cold-mind-games-with-jets/

COACH BILL BELICHICK FUN FACT #50

THE PATRIOT WAY | UNACTIONABLE ANALYTICS AND DATA IS A WASTE OF TIME

Coach Bill Belichick does not want to fill his mind with in-actionable data and technology.

https://www.boston.com/sports/new-england-patriots/2019/09/27/bill-belichick-analytics-patriots-bills

COACH BILL BELICHICK FUN FACT #51

BILL HAS RECEIVED BOTH AN HONORARY DOCTORATE FROM WESLEYAN UNIVERSITY AS WELL AS WESLEYAN UNIVERSITY'S BALDWIN MEDAL

Although Wesleyan University has elected to not rename the school as Coach Bill Belichick University (as of the time this book has been written), Coach Bill Belichick received incredible honors from the University where he attended school. Coach Bill Belichick has both an honorary doctorate from Wesleyan as well as the university's Baldwin Medal, the highest honor awarded to an alumnus for distinguished achievement.

Coach Bill Belichick began his National Football League coaching career immediately after he graduated from Wesleyan. Coach Bill Belichick, is the son of Steve Belichick, a former longtime assistant football coach with the U.S. Naval Academy, earned his first NFL job with the Baltimore Colts during the year of 1975. While Coach Bill Belichick attended Wesleyan University which is located in Middletown, Connecticut, he played both center and tight end for the school's football team. While playing football for the college team, played both lacrosse and squash, where he led as the captain of the lacrosse team during his senior season at Wesleyan University. Coach Bill Belichick was a member of Chi Psi fraternity during his time at Wesleyan University. Belichick earned his college bachelor's degree in economics in 1975 from Wesleyan University. Coach Bill Belichick was actually part of the inaugural induction class into Wesleyan University's Athletics Hall of Fame during the spring of 2008.

COACH BILL BELICHICK FUN FACT #52

THE PATRIOT WAY |
COACH BILL BELICHICK HAS BUILT A TEAM
AROUND HIM TO MINIMIZE DISTRACTIONS

Coach Bill Belichick is obsessive about creating an environment where distractions are minimized and where he can focus on willing games, recruiting players and coaching players.

https://www.nytimes.com/2012/02/04/sports/football/berj-najarian-is-a-key-figure-in-the-patriots-inner-circle.html

COACH BILL BELICHICK FUN FACT #53

THE PATRIOT WAY | COACH BILL BELICHICK
IS IN DANGER OF RUNNING OUT OF
FINGERS FOR SUPER BOWL RINGS

Bill Wearing All 8 Rings:

pic.twitter.com/IzGNzmMkjV

https://nesn.com/2019/06/bill-belichick-in-danger-of-running-out-of-fingers-for-super-bowl-rings/

COACH BILL BELICHICK FUN FACT #54

THE PATRIOT WAY | MORE PLAYOFF WINS THAN THE CARDINALS, BROWNS AND LIONS HAVE HAD IN THEIR COMBINED 231 SEASONS OF EXISTENCE IN THE LEAGUE

Belichick and the Tom Brady Patriots have earned more playoff wins in 17 seasons than the Cardinals, Browns, and Lions have put up in their combined 231 seasons of existence in the league.

COACH BILL BELICHICK FUN FACT #55

THE PATRIOT WAY | FIRST ALL-TIME IN PLAYOFF COACHING WINS

https://en.m.wikipedia.org/wiki/Stephen_Belichick

Belichick was the NFL's longest-tenured head coach, as well as the first all-time in playoff coaching wins, second in regular season coaching wins in the NFL. He is one of only three coaches who have won six titles.

COACHES WITH 6 TITLES:

- **Coach Bill Belichick** –

- **George Halas** – He was the founder, owner, and head coach of the National Football League's Chicago Bears

- **Curly Lambeau** – From 1919 to 1949, Lambeau was the head coach and general manager of the Packers. He led his team to over 200 wins and six NFL championships, including three consecutive wins from 1929 to 1931. He shares the distinction with rival George Halas of the Chicago Bears and later, Coach Bill Belichick of the New England Patriots of coaching his team to the most NFL championships.

COACH BILL BELICHICK FUN FACT #56

THE PATRIOT WAY |
PRACTICE UNTIL YOU CAN'T GET IT WRONG

"I think practice preparation is always an indicator of game performance — not necessarily 100%, because there are still a lot of variables there, but it's still an indicator."

- COACH BILL BELICHICK

https://www.cnbc.com/2017/04/13/bill-belichick-leadership-rules.html

COACH BILL BELICHICK FUN FACT #57

THE PATRIOT WAY | DEPENDABILITY IS
COACH BILL BELICHICK'S FAVORITE ABILITY

> "It's not all about talent. It's about dependability, consistency, and being able to improve. If you work hard and you're coachable, and you understand what you need to do, you can improve."
>
> - COACH BILL BELICHICK

https://www.cnbc.com/2017/04/13/bill-belichick-leadership-rules.html

> "Talent sets the floor, character sets the ceiling."
>
> – COACH BILL BELICHICK

https://sportsforthesoul.com/bill-belichick-6-lessons-success/

COACH BILL BELICHICK FUN FACT #58

THE PATRIOT WAY |
COACH BILL BELICHICK DOES NOT
MIND BEING DISLIKED

Through Coach Bill Belichick's legendary career, he has the habit of making decisions that are correct and often unpopular.

https://touchdownwire.usatoday.com/2018/01/25/tom-brady-new-england-patriots-super-bowl-lii-record-stats-facts-record-belichick/2/

NOTABLE QUOTABLE

....

"It is much safer to be feared than loved because ...love is preserved by the link of obligation which, owing to the baseness of men, is broken at every opportunity for their advantage; but fear preserves you by a dread of punishment which never fails."

— Niccolò Machiavelli

(May 3rd 1469 – June 21st 1527) - Machiavelli was a Florentine diplomat, author, philosopher, and historian who lived during the Italian Renaissance. Niccolò Machiavelli best known for his political treatise The Prince (Il Principe), written around 1513 but not published until 1532, five years after his death. He has often been called the father of modern political philosophy and political science.

COACH BILL BELICHICK FUN FACT #59

THE PATRIOT WAY | WINNING IS A HABIT FOR COACH BILL BELICHICK

At 49 Consecutive Years, Coach Bill Belichick Owns the Record for the number of Consecutive Years Working As Coach In Some Capacity In the NFL

https://www.boston.com/sports/new-england-patriots/2024/01/11/bill-belichick-records-stats-wins-seasons-history-timeline/

THE PATRIOT WAY | BRADY AND BELICHICK TOGETHER ARE REWRITING THE SUPER BOWL RECORD BOOKS

https://www.sbnation.com/nfl/2019/2/3/18207599/tom-brady-super-bowl-records-patriots

» Most games played (9)
» Most wins (6)
» Most passing touchdowns, career (18)
» Most passing yards, career (2,838) (more than the next two closest combined)
» Most passing yards in a game (505)
» Oldest quarterback to win a Super Bowl (41)
» Most 300-yard passing games (4)
» Most passes without an interception, game (48)
» Most pass completions, career (256) (65.3% completion rate)
» Most passes completed, game (43) (He also holds the second and fourth most record as well)

THE PATRIOT WAY | BILL COACHED THE 199TH PICK IN THE 2000 DRAFT TO BECOME ONE OF THE BEST QUARTERBACKS OF ALL TIME

With the 199th pick of the 2000 NFL draft, Coach Bill Belichick drafted Tom Brady.

https://www.sbnation.com/nfl/2019/2/3/18207599/tom-brady-super-bowl-records-patriots

COACH BILL BELICHICK FUN FACT #62

THE PATRIOT WAY | BEFORE JOINING THE UNIVERSITY OF NORTH CAROLINA, COACH BILL BELICHICK WAS NOT ON SOCIAL MEDIA.

"I'm not on SnapFace and all those ... I'm not too worried about what they put on InstantChat."

— COACH BILL BELICHICK

https://www.thrivetimeshow.com/business-podcasts/bill-belichick-facts-part-5-a-look-under-the-hoodie-exploring-102-facts-about-the-management-mastery-of-coach-bill-belichick/

https://www.facebook.com/watch/?v=10154704007996263

COACH BILL BELICHICK FUN FACT #63

THE PATRIOT WAY | BRADY / BELICHICK ARE BETTER THAN 47 FIRST ROUND DRAFT PICK QUARTERBACKS COMBINED

https://www.sbnation.com/nfl/2019/2/3/18207599/tom-brady-super-bowl-records-patriots

COACH BILL BELICHICK FUN FACT #64

THE PATRIOT WAY | BILL HAS BEEN IN 8 SUPER BOWLS IN 17 YEARS

https://www.sbnation.com/nfl/2019/2/3/18207599/tom-brady-super-bowl-records-patriots

COACH BILL BELICHICK FUN FACT #65

ALL-TIME COACHING RECORD

As a Three-time Associated Press NFL Coach of the Year (2003, 2007, 2010), Coach Bill Belichick Has An All-Time NFL Head Coaching record of 333-178 (. 652) and Is Only 14 NFL Wins Away from the Overall Wins Record (As of January 1st 2025)

COACH BILL BELICHICK FUN FACT #66

THE PATRIOT WAY | BILL KNOWS THE NFL RULE BOOK INSIDE AND OUT.

"Patriots Coach Bill Belichick is widely hailed as a rule book master. He knows what's allowed, what's pushing the envelope and what obscure rule he can use to his advantage that the other coach never even considered."

-Jonathan Jones (November 18th 2016, Sports Illustrated)

READ - https://www.si.com/nfl/2016/11/18/nfl-rule-book-bill-belichick-richard-sherman

BOSTON (CBS) — Coach Bill Belichick knows a few things. For one, he knows the NFL rule book inside and out, better than just about anybody else on the planet. That knowledge has certainly aided him during this 20-year stretch of NFL dominance.

https://boston.cbslocal.com/2019/10/22/bill-belichick-exploits-loophole-expects-nfl-to-close-it-patriots-jets/

COACH BILL BELICHICK FUN FACT #67

THE PATRIOT WAY | BILL LOVES EXPLOITING LOOPHOLES IN THE RULE BOOK

https://boston.cbslocal.com/2019/10/22/bill-belichick-exploits-loophole-expects-nfl-to-close-it-patriots-jets/

https://www.businessinsider.com/how-google-retains-more-than-90-of-market-share-2018-4

COACH BILL BELICHICK FUN FACT #68

DEPENDABILITY MATTERS MOST TO COACH BILL BELICHICK

"We like to say that dependability is more important than ability." - Coach Bill Belichick

THE PATRIOT WAY | HOW BILL CHOOSES TO DEAL WITH REPORTERS

https://www.nbcsports.com/boston/patriots/bill-belichick-talks-relationship-media-when-reporters-cross-line

"Belichick certainly sets the bar in Boston when it comes to keeping the media at arm's length. But at least he's willing to admit where he draws his battle lines." - Darren Hartwell

https://www.nbcsportsboston.com/nfl/new-england-patriots/bill-belichick-talks-relationship-with-media-when-reporters-cross-the-line/379898/

THE PATRIOT WAY | BILL HAS EARNED 8 SUPER BOWL RINGS THAT HE DOES NOT WEAR

https://sportsworld.nbcsports.com/everyones-got-a-bill-belichick-story/

Belichick fact: He keeps his eight Super Bowl rings (two with the Giants, six with the Patriots) in a box somewhere—he does not wear them, and whenever a media person asks him about them he dismisses them.

COACH BILL BELICHICK FUN FACT #71

THE PATRIOT WAY | PLAYERS WILL TAKE LESS TO LEARN FROM THE BEST

https://sportsworld.nbcsports.com/everyones-got-a-bill-belichick-story/

Rodney Harrison was heading out to Oakland to talk to the Raiders about a job. He was 30 years old, a free agent, a two-time Pro Bowl safety, and many felt like he had seen his best days. Harrison had already talked with Denver, and he had all but decided to sign with the Broncos. Then his phone rang. It was Coach Bill Belichick.

The two talked for only a few minutes. Belichick said the Patriots wanted him. They didn't need to talk to him in person. They didn't need to check out if he was healthy. They just wanted him. Harrison was curious why.

"I saw you in warmups one time, and I saw you level a wide receiver," Belichick said.

"You saw that?" Harrison asked in wonderment. He remembered the exact moment Belichick was talking about. A teammate was running over the middle in a drill, and Harrison knocked him down hard. He did get fired up for football.

"Yeah," Belichick said. "And I knew right then that I wanted you to play for us."

"After we hung up," Harrison says, "I called my agent and told him, 'I don't care what you have to do, I don't care how much money we have to leave on the table, I want to play for Coach Bill Belichick ... I probably could have gotten a million dollars more a year with Denver. But after he said that... what other coach would even be watching a drill? And who else would remember that? I knew. I had to play for Coach Bill Belichick."

COACH BILL BELICHICK FUN FACT #72

THE PATRIOT WAY | BILL MAKES PRACTICE HARDER THAN THE GAMES

"My personal coaching philosophy, my mentality has always been to make things as difficult as possible for players in practice, however bad we can make them, I make them."

- COACH BILL BELICHICK

COACH BILL BELICHICK FUN FACT #73

THE PATRIOT WAY | BILL LOVES OVERACHIEVERS INCLUDING CHARLES BARKLEY

https://sportsworld.nbcsports.com/everyones-got-a-bill-belichick-story/

Belichick fact: Coach Bill Belichick loves Charles Barkley. He has loved Barkley going back to when he was coaching in Cleveland and Barkley was playing for the Philadelphia 76ers. It boggled his mind that Barkley, at 6-foot-6 or less, could lead the NBA in rebounding. That is the sort of magic that leaves Coach Bill Belichick awed.

COACH BILL BELICHICK FUN FACT #74

THE PATRIOT WAY | A MAN OF VERY FEW WORDS

https://sportsworld.nbcsports.com/everyones-got-a-bill-belichick-story/

A story: Jonathan Vilma and his college teammate D.J. Williams were scheduled to work out for Belichick down in Miami. They were both big-time prospects – both would end up first-round picks – and the Patriots had two picks in the 2004 first round. So this was an important workout. Belichick showed up with his son Steve and said two words:

"Hi guys."

"Then he worked us out for the maximum time allowed," Vilma says. "I mean: To the minute. At the end we were dog-tired, sweating, we had worked and worked. ... And as soon as we stopped he said, 'All right guys.' And he walked off.

"We were just standing there, and we looked at each other like: 'Did that just happen?' Our agent called – we had the same agent – and he asked: 'How did it go?' And we just said, 'No idea. He didn't say anything to us.'"

Vilma and Williams were both off the board when Belichick and the Patriots selected, but New England did select another Miami teammate, Vince Wilfork. Vilma went to the Jets where he won defensive rookie of the year. But when they played the Patriots, he noticed that Belichick never said a word to him. They would cross paths – Vilma would go talk with Wilfork – but he never said a word.

In 2009, Vilma was a Pro Bowler with New Orleans and they played the Patriots, and he had a spectacular game. One more time, after the game, he saw Wilfork next to Belichick. The coach did not say a word to him.

The next year, at training camp, the Saints and Patriots had a practice. Vilma was warming up and, suddenly –"out of nowhere," in Vilma's memory – Belichick just appears behind him.

"I'm glad you're out of my division," Belichick said, without any words of introduction.

"Thanks coach," Vilma said hesitantly.

"No, I'm serious," Belichick said. "You're a hell of a player."

"No smile, no nothing," Vilma says now as he remembers. "He just said it so matter of factly. And that's it. He walked away."

THE PATRIOT WAY | BILL IS 100% ON 100% OF THE TIME

https://sportsworld.nbcsports.com/everyones-got-a-bill-belichick-story/

Gonzalez played in 14 Pro Bowls – he loved playing when it was in Hawaii. Things were always so relaxing there, so fun. One year, Belichick was his coach, and Gonzalez was curious what made this guy so good. Great players are as bedazzled by Coach Bill Belichick's magic as anyone else. They have all played for good coaches. They have heard all the inspirational stories, all been screamed at for not doing something right, all been shown something on tape that perfectly foreshadowed what they would see in the game. What's so different about this guy?

On the opening kickoff, Gonzalez was out on special teams – there are no backup players at the Pro Bowl, so the stars have to do some menial things – and he went through the motions and didn't block anybody. Gonzalez jogged happily to the sidelines.

"Why don't you (bleeping) block somebody Gonzalez," Belichick grumbled as Gonzalez jogged by.

What? Did he just say that? Gonzalez turned and Belichick was just glaring at him, "like I was a piece of dirt."

Gonzalez felt himself fuming. This was how the great Coach Bill Belichick treated people? They were at the Pro Bowl, for crying out loud. This was Hawaii, for crying out loud. It was a beautiful day, blue sky, blue water, this was supposed to be a reward, a way to honor Gonzalez for working absurdly hard and having another extraordinary season. And this was what he gets? To have the game's most famous coach swear at him for not blocking on special teams in an exhibition game?

Oh, yes, he was mad – who did this guy think he was? Gonzalez played football the right way. He didn't deserve this. He stewed on the sideline, furious. Then it was time to go back on the field for another kickoff, another special teams moment, and the ball was kicked. Gonzalez locked in on a guy running down the field. "Why don't you (bleeping) block somebody?" Sure, he heard it again. OK coach, fine, check out this block.

Gonzalez absolutely mashed the defender, took him completely out of the play.

Then Gonzalez walked over to the sideline, and you better believe he walked right by Belichick. He wanted to see the grimace wiped right off the man's face. But Belichick showed no signs of even noticing him. He was looking out on the field, seemingly oblivious to Gonzalez's presence. So Gonzalez kept walking. And as he was a few steps away, he heard Coach Bill Belichick say this:

"Nice block, Gonzalez."

He looked back, and there was no hint of a smile on Belichick's face. Coach Bill Belichick just kept looking at the field, and in that moment Tony Gonzalez understood. The man had coached him into blocking on special teams in the Pro Bowl.

COACH BILL BELICHICK FUN FACT #76

THE PATRIOT WAY |
COACH BILL BELICHICK HAS READ
ALL OF THE HARRY POTTER BOOKS!

https://sportsworld.nbcsports.com/everyones-got-a-bill-belichick-story/

Coach Bill Belichick loves the Grateful Dead and Bon Jovi, will quote "The Art of War," has read all the Harry Potter books, preferred lacrosse to football as a player and is probably breaking down film right now, no matter when you are reading this.

Top Time Wasting Activities:

- Social Media – Average person spends 11.3 hours per day on media – https://www. nielsen.com/us/en/insights/article/2018/ time-flies-us-adults-now-spend-nearly- half-a-day-interacting-with-media/

- Religious Debates –

- Political Debates –

COACH BILL BELICHICK FUN FACT #77

THE PATRIOT WAY | COACH BILL BELICHICK CONSISTENTLY QUOTES "THE ART OF WAR"

Because Coach Bill Belichick's father and mentor Steve Belichick, was a coach at the United States Naval Academy for 34 years, it should not come as a surprise that Coach Bill Belichick would draw inspiration from text related to military strategy. Bill Belichick's father, Coach Steve Belichick also developed an incredible and massive library of historical football books which a young Coach Bill Belichick devoured and grew up around. Coach Bill Belichick's perspective of the overall game of football was thus undoubtedly influenced by legendary football coaches such as Walter Camp, Vince Lombardi and Knute Rockne.

Coach Bill Belichick is legendary for the endless strategic planning he invests into preparing the gameplan and his team for each and every game. In fact, in order to keep his Patriots teams focused Coach Bill Belichick relies on a key quote on the wall that he keeps posted where his players can constantly see it.

"The only sign we have in the locker room is from 'The Art of War.' 'Every battle is won before it is fought,'" he told CNBC contributor Suzy Welch in 2017. -

https://www.cnbc.com/2019/01/31/bill-belichick-uses-this-sun-tzu-quote-to-inspire-the-patriots-to-win.html

"I think if you want to go far enough, look at Sun Tzu... Look at the great generals, you exploit your strengths and attack weaknesses. That's about as fundamental as it gets. If there's something that you can do well, you want to try to do it. If there is something that your opponent is weak at, you want to try to attack it, and if you can match those up, then that's a good way of attack...If you can find a way to use your strengths without them knowing exactly what you're doing, or you have some little bit of disguise or distraction to it, then, I think, fundamentally, that's really what you try to do...Be sound, play to your strengths and attack the opponent's weaknesses. Again, that's a much longer, detailed conversation, but at the heart of it, that's really where it starts for us every week. What do we need to stop, and what can we do, and then build it from there."

https://www.patriots.com/news/notebook-belichick-traces-flexible-game-plan-approach-back-to-sun-tzu-s-art-of-w

COACH BILL BELICHICK FUN FACT #78

THE PATRIOT WAY | BILL WILL ALWAYS FIND ROOM FOR IMPROVEMENT ESPECIALLY ON WINNING GAMES

In 2011, after successfully coaching one of the most successful offensive games in the history of professional football, Coach Bill Belichick found room for himself and his team to improve.

Although quarterback Tom Brady threw for a mind-blowing 517 yards and the Patriots offense earned 622 yards in a Monday night 38-24 victory over the Miami Dolphins, Coach Bill Belichick was still looking for areas in which his offense could improve.

In fact during the Tuesday press conference that followed the game, Coach Bill Belichick said the following: "We had the ball on the 1-yard line ready to score a touchdown and we end up getting knocked out of field goal range and couldn't get a field goal before the half."

Coach Bill Belichick also took the time to share that he was not in favor of the way the game ended either.

Coach Bill Belichick stated, "We really weren't able to close out the game. At the end of the game there were a couple of first downs that we couldn't make. The good thing was, offensively, whenever Miami scored or started to change the momentum of the game a little bit, our offense was able to come back and drive the ball and score points and change that momentum around, so that was great."

Throughout the game, Tom Brady largely led the team with a no-huddle offense, which prevented the Miami Dolphins from being able to make the player substitutions that they wanted to make.

Coach Belichick commented during Tuesday's press conference following the Monday night victory, "It's great that we could take advantage of it, but those opportunities won't always be there...I'm sure as teams get more experienced with their communication and get further into the season, you'll see less and less of that...We're just trying to keep ironing out all the little details and that's really across the board. It's offense, defense, special teams. There are always things on every play, even good plays, that a lot of times aren't done quite properly and had the (opposing) defense or the offense been in (a) different play or done things a little bit differently, then we would have had a problem."

During this incredible offensive performance by Coach Bill Belichick's Patriots, Tom Brady threw four touchdowns, two of which went to Wes Welker, and tight ends, Aaron Hernandez and Rob Gronkowski.

https://www.masslive.com/patriots/2011/09/bill_belichick_sees_room_for_i.html

COACH BILL BELICHICK FUN FACT #79

THE PATRIOT WAY | BILL WAS PRESIDENT OF THE CHI PSI FRATERNITY AT WESLEYAN UNIVERSITY

Although Coach Bill Belichick is known for his determined and stoic demeanor he does occasionally publicly show a sense of humor and emotion. However, before he became known as the stoic and determined coaching icon, he was the president of the hard-partying Chi Psi fraternity at Wesleyan University. Many have described the Chi Psi fraternity as a real-life Animal House. While attending

Wesleyan University Coach Bill Belichick was very much involved in college athletics. In fact, during his time at college, Coach Bill Belichick played squash, lacrosse and football.

According to Mike Celeste who played football and lacrosse with Coach Bill Belichick during college, "We were Animal House before the movie. It seemed like we were on double-secret probation the whole time."

https://www.sportscasting.com/news/bill-belichick-was-once-the-president-of-a-hard-partying-college-fraternity/

COACH BILL BELICHICK FUN FACT #80

THE PATRIOT WAY | COACH BILL BELICHICK SENT OUT 250 HAND WRITTEN LETTERS TO COLLEGE COACHES TO TRY AND OBTAIN HIS FIRST JOB

Although Coach Bill Belichick is now known as a legendary NFL coach he had to start somewhere. Thus, in order to secure his first coaching job the 22-year-old Coach Bill Belichick mailed out nearly 250 hand-written letters asking for a coaching job. Coach Belichick landed his first coaching job working as an assistant for Baltimore Colts head coach Ted Marchibroda in 1975. After Coach Bill Belichick was interviewed by head coach Ted Marchibroda, Bill Belichick told Coach Marchibroda that he was willing to work 14-16 hours a day, and that he'd do anything his boss asked of him. Coach Marchibroda thought that Bill

Belichick sounded like he was being sincere and decided to hire Coach Bill Belichick. Coach Bill Belichick's first job involved breaking down copious amounts of game film, driving the coaches around when they needed a ride, working the Xerox machine and $25 per week, which was $21.22 after taxes. Coach Bill Belichick fondly remembers those days by stating, "I got three meals, a bed, and a lot of football," he told O'Connor, "and that was all I really wanted at the time...a graduate course in football."

https://www.cnbc.com/2019/01/31/bill-belichick-got-his-first-nfl-job-at-23-it-paid-25-dollars-a-week.html https://www.businessinsider.com/bill-belichick-coaching-career-2016-1

NOTABLE QUOTABLE

....

"Success is the ability to go from one failure to another with no loss of enthusiasm." – Winston Churchhill (on financial education and entrepreneurship

"People who do not succeed have one distinguishing trait in common. They know all the reasons for failure, and have what they believe to be air-tight alibis to explain their own lack of achievement:

» If I had the money
» If I could get the job
» If I had been given
  a chance
» If I were only younger
» If I were only older
» If I only had a better
  education
» If I could just save
  some money
» If I lived in a big city
» If I were not so fat
» If my talents were known

» If I didn't have a past   » If I had the courage"

» If I had my own business

—Napoleon Hill (on personal development)

COACH BILL BELICHICK FUN FACT #81

THE PATRIOT WAY | COACH BILL BELICHICK CHOOSES TO LIVE IN HINGHAM, MASSACHUSETTS

Coach Bill Belichick purchased his home in 2006, which is located in Hingham, Massachusetts. The home is 3500 square feet with three bedrooms and four bathrooms. Coach Bill Belichick also owns a number of properties and homes located on the island of Nantucket, Massachusetts. Coach Bill Belichick has been purchasing properties in this area since the year 1979. Hingham, Massachusetts is a small town located in northern Plymouth County, Massachusetts. This area is considered to be part of the Great Boston area and is located on the South Shore of Massachusetts. When the 2020 census was conducted the town reported a total population of 24,284 people. The town was named after Hingham, Norfolk, England and was originally settled back in 1633 by English colonists.

https://www.si.com/onsi/athlete-lifestyle/real-estate/bill-belichick-s-massachusetts-home-is-surprisingly-small

https://www.si.com/onsi/athlete-lifestyle/real-estate/bill-belichick-s-massachusetts-home-is-surprisingly-small#:~:text=Belichick%20purchased%20the%20Hingham%2C%20Massachusetts,Here's%20a%20view%20of%20it.

COACH BILL BELICHICK FUN FACT #82

THE PATRIOT WAY | COACH BILL BELICHICK HAS EARNED EIGHT SUPER BOWL RINGS

To most NFL enthusiasts and the coaching community, Coach Belichick is known as the greatest coach in the history of professional sports as he has now won a total of eight Super Bowls. Coach Bill Belichick earned six of his Super Bowl victories while serving as the head coach for the New England Patriots and two of his Super Bowl victories while serving as an assistant coach for the New York Giants. Coach Bill Belichick also is ranked number one among National Football League coaches with 31 playoff wins.

https://www.espn.com/nfl/story/_/id/39286200/best-nfl-coaches-all-ranked-wins

COACH BILL BELICHICK FUN FACT #83

THE PATRIOT WAY | COACH BILL BELICHICK OWNS A DOG, WHICH IS AN ALASKAN KLEE KAI

According to many in the dog industry, near the time of the increased interest in the demand for the Klee Kai breed of dogs, Coach Bill Belichick's dog was attentively sitting at attention at the kitchen table behind Coach Belichick's computer while the New England Patriots were finalizing their first draft pick of the 2020 draft. According to sources, Coach Bill Belichick's dog, "Nike" saw many leftover treats that were sitting on the table and decided to hop up onto the chair to wait patiently for a reward from Coach Bill Belichick.

https://www.si.com/nfl/2020/05/29/bill-belichick-dog-alaskan-klee-kai-demand-surge#:~:text=Bill%20Belichick's%20Alaskan%20Klee%20Kai,that%20now%20everyone%20wants%20one.

COACH BILL BELICHICK FUN FACT #84

THE PATRIOT WAY | COACH BILL BELICHICK'S FULL NAME IS WILLIAM STEPHEN BELICHICK

Coach Bill Belichick was born with the birth name, William Stephen Belichick on April 16, 1952, in beautiful Nashville, Tennessee. Coach Bill Belichick is the only child of Coach Steve Belichick and non-coach Jeannette Belichick. Coach Bill Belichick showed an interest for the game of football at a very young age, which many say he inherited from his father who was a longtime assistant football coach and college football scout.

https://www.biography.com/athletes/a91277838/bill-belichick

COACH BILL BELICHICK FUN FACT #85

THE PATRIOT WAY | COACH BILL BELICHICK WAS HIRED AT NORTH CAROLINA TO REPLACE MACK BROWN AS THE NEXT TAR HEEL'S FOOTBALL COACH

Coach Bill Belichick decided to become a college football coach for the first time in 2024.

North Carolina made the decision to hire Coach Bill Belichick to replace Mack Brown as the next Tar Heels' next college football coach. Despite being just 14 wins away from breaking the all-time wins record set by NFL legend, Don Shula, Coach Belichick has reported to be very enthusiastic about coaching at the University of North Carolina. During the press conference where North Carolina announced the hiring of Coach Bill Belichick, Coach Bill Belichick chose to describe his new coaching position as a "Dream come true."

https://www.usatoday.com/story/sports/ncaaf/2024/12/12/bill-belichick-unc-football-coach-live-updates/76941983007/

COACH BILL BELICHICK #86

ONE OF THE FIRST TIMES COACH BELICHICK HAS BEEN REMEMBERED FOR WEARING HIS ICONIC HOODIE WAS DURING A 2003 FOOTBALL GAME AGAINST THE DALLAS COWBOYS

During 2003, in a game where Coach Bill Belichick coached against the Dallas Cowboys, this was the first time that many Coach Bill Belichick fans remember Coach Belichick wearing his iconic and legendary gray hoodie. During this game, Coach Bill Belichick was coaching against his former boss and mentor Coach Bill Parcells for the first time since Coach Bill Belichick chose to not succeed Coach Bill Parcells as the next head coach of the New York Jets. Leading up to this game, the media created alot of hype about this Coach Bill Parcells versus Coach Bill Belichick matchup and thus all eyes were on Coach Bill Belichick and his grey hoodie. Coach Belichick told WEEI radio about why he chose to wear the grey hoodie, "In all honesty, I really don't pay that much attention to it, I swear I don't. People ask me after the game, 'Why did you wear the blue one? Why did you wear the gray one?' I just put on whatever is there."

https://www.espn.com/espn/feature/story/_/id/30161649/bill-belichick-hoodies-explained-visual-history-new-england-patriots-coach-most-memorable-looks#:~:text=The%20hoodie%20has%20since%20taken,you%20wear%20the%20blue%20one%3F

COACH BILL BELICHICK FUN FACT #87

COACH BILL BELICHICK FUN FACT #86 | TOM BRADY IS FOREVER GRATEFUL FOR COACH BILL BELICHICK

Although the debate rages on as to whether Coach Bill Belichick could have won his 6 Super Bowls without the help of quarterback Tom Brady, it is a fact that Tom Brady would more than likely not have been drafted without Coach Bill Belichick. It is also a fact that Tom Brady was coachable and Coach Bill Belichick is an incredible coach. Tom Brady stated, "I could never have been the player I was without you Coach Belichick. I am forever grateful. And I wish you the best of luck in whatever you choose next."

https://www.cbsnews.com/boston/news/bill-belichick-leaving-new-england-patriots-tom-brady-reaction/

COACH BILL BELICHICK FUN FACT #88

COACH BILL BELICHICK IS FRIENDS WITH COACHING LEGEND NICK SABAN

Coach Bill Belichick and Coach Nick Saban are known as two of the greatest head coaches to have ever coached the game of football. Coach Bill Belichick has won an incredible six Super Bowls as a National Football League head coach and Coach Nick Saban has won a mind-blowing seven championships as a college coach. For over 40 years Coach Bill Belichick and Coach Nick Saban have maintained a friendship. In fact, in 1982 Coach Nick Saban was hired at the Naval Academy where Coach Bill Belichick's father, Steve Belichick was working as an assistant football coach. Coach Nick Saban and Coach Bill Belichick's friendship began when Coach Bill Belichick returned home to visit his family and the two have stayed close ever since that time. Just a few short years later, Coach Bill Belichick was hired to be the head coach of the Cleveland Browns. After being hired as the head coach of the Cleveland Browns, Coach Bill Belichick knew right away who he was going to hire to be his defensive coordinator.

> "Nick was the first coach I hired and the best coach I hired. He was really my number one partner there, and I had tremendous confidence in him at every level."
>
> - COACH BILL BELICHICK

https://www.sportskeeda.com/college-football/
is-bill-belichick-friends-nick-saban-exploring-
relationship-legendary-football-coaches

COACH BILL BELICHICK NEVER DELEGATES THE JOB OF WATCHING FILM TO SOMEBODY ELSE BECAUSE THAT IS HOW YOU WIN

A man by the name of Phil Savage had the pleasure of working for the legend, Coach Bill Belichick while Coach Bill Belichick was serving as the head coach of the Cleveland Browns. Phil Savage who worked for Coach Bill Belichick from 1993 to 1993 invested the time to share what it was like to actually watch game film with Coach Bill Belichick with ESPN Magazine:

"My film breakdowns weren't what he wanted. So he says, 'Let's just sit down and go through a few plays together.' We're getting ready for Tampa, he throws the first play up on the screen and starts going, from the inside out, over every single tiny detail. 'See this split of the linemen? That's 2 feet. That's 3 feet. That one's 2 feet between the center and the guard. Write that down. OK, now look at the splits of the wide receivers. The Z is inside the numbers. The X is outside. OK, the quarterback. Look! Right there! He looks to the left, to the right, to the left, then to the middle and then he hikes the ball. You gotta monitor that because it could help our defensive linemen get a jump on the snap.'"

"He proceeds to go through all these little intricacies on the game film ... and it's 20 minutes on one play. Twenty minutes! In my immature mind I'm sitting there in the dark doing the math: Three games to break down on each side of the ball, 60 plays in each game, 20 minutes a play means I can get through three plays in an hour. My god, I'll never sleep again. And I didn't."

https://patriotswire.usatoday.com/2016/10/08/whats-it-like-to-watchgame-film-with-bill-belichick-a-former-coaching-assistant-explains/

Coach Bill Belichick has described his approach to watching NFL game film: "You can really get to everything, between the different angles, the TV copy, and so many different ways to look at plays...Before, when I came into the league, you had the film. You had one, kind of look at it. If you want to cut out plays, like short yardage, third down, or something like that, you could do that. It was a little bit of trouble, but you could do it...The concept now of looking at...it's really limitless the way you can put all that together and how quickly it can come together, so it gives you a lot of options...You can get caught in the weeds with so many little details and all that...I think you've just got to be careful that you don't miss the big picture. It does provide for some very detailed analysis.

If you want to watch a specific type of player against another specific type of player, if you want to watch a certain tackle against two or three speed rushers on pass plays, you can pull those plays in ten seconds. That would've taken a month to do when I first came into the league... With a larger staff, we kind of divide that up so we can get into it a little bit deeper look, a deeper dive into some of that. Again, the archives that you can keep are pretty amazing as well. If you want to look at all the reverses in the last 10 years, they'll be ready for you in a very short amount of time. It's a great resource and figuring out the best way to manage it, use it, is really the challenge."

COACH BILL BELICHICK FUN FACT #90

SOME CONSIDER COACH BILL BELICHICK TO BE A COACHING GENIUS

The skill, the talent, the enigma and the greatness that is Coach Bill Belichick comes from his ability to focus obsessively on one thing, winning football games. Coach Bill Belichick has developed a method, and processes for identifying talent that other teams do not see and developing that talent into a championship winning team. He is known throughout the football universe as being the master coach who taught Tom Brady how to become a great quarterback, the man who created a framework that allowed Randy Moss to thrive again, the guru who created an offense where Wes Welker could win, the wizard who developed an offense where Julian Edelman could dominate, the defensive chess player who created a defense that allowed Lawrence Taylor to fully utilize his skillset, the mastermind who created a dual tight end offense that allowed Aaron Hernandez and Rob Gronkowski to become unstoppable and more.

https://www.nytimes.com/2024/01/12/opinion/bill-belichick-patriots-football.html#:~:text=The%20genius%20of%20Belichick%20rests,greatest%20player%20of%20all%20time.

COACH BILL BELICHICK FUN FACT #91

COACH BILL BELICHICK IS THE INNOVATOR BEHIND THE CONCEPT OF CUTTING OFF THE SLEEVES OF HOODIE SWEATSHIRTS

Coach Bill Belichick dropped knowledge bombs when describing why he decided to lead the movement by spearheading the fashion concept of cutting the sleeves off of a hoodie sweatshirt. "It's comfortable. I carry stuff in my pouch," he said. As for chopping off the sleeves, I have short arms."

https://www.espn.com/espn/feature/story/_/id/30161649/bill-belichick-hoodies-explained-visual-history-new-england-patriots-coach-most-memorable-looks#:~:text=%22It's%20comfortable.,%22I%20have%20short%20arms.%22

COACH BILL BELICHICK FUN FACT #92

COACH BILL BELICHICK CHOOSING TO BRING HIS COACHING TALENTS TO THE UNIVERSITY OF NORTH CAROLINA AT CHAPEL HILL WILL FOREVER CHANGE THE WAY COLLEGE FOOTBALL IS COACHED

With the hiring of Coach Bill Belichick, it is becoming increasingly obvious that college football is becoming more and more like professional football. More and more colleges are hiring general managers to help their college programs with their focus being on recruiting the best talent they can find while finding a way to finance the importation of the talent. Because college football now allows athletes to be compensated for the use of their name, image and likeness, players can now be paid by brands and other forms of sponsorship.

In past years, college athletes were also very limited when it came to transferring to other college programs throughout their collegiate playing career. However, players can now freely transfer to other teams due to the creation of the transfer portal window which was reduced in October of 2024 to 30 days for Division I basketball and football players. Because of these rule changes and other dynamics, college coaches must now learn how to keep their players happy, while coaching them, recruiting outside talent, and retaining the talent they want to keep. In fact, one could argue that the free agency of college athletes is more free than that of professional athletes in 2025.

Coach Bill Belichick described his approach to coaching at the college level as, "We're just selling our program and it's a pro program...We'll develop the players professionally to play football, and if that leads them there and if they're talented enough, either way we're developing pros. We have my strength coach from New England, my chef from New England, coaches from pro football, and so we train and we prepare and do everything in a pro football program and that's going to translate to for the players, that they'll learn that. And [if] they have enough talent to go into the NFL they'll be ready to go, and if they go in another direction, which eventually all athletes do—you can't play forever—then they'll be trained to go into life and their chosen profession, and learn the things about leadership, discipline and structure they need to be productive."

https://www.si.com/college-football/bill-belichick-explains-how-nfl-prepared-him-college-recruiting

COACH BILL BELICHICK FUN FACT #93

THE PATRIOT WAY |
COACH BILL BELICHICK LOVES COACHING

"I like what I am doing. I enjoy all parts of the game – the team building, training camp, game days, the excitement of Sunday... it beats working."

– COACH BILL BELICHICK

Want to love your job as much as Coach Bill Belichick loves his?

» Create decor that makes you want to come to work more.

» Get intentional about the sites in your office

» De-Prioritize money earnings as your top priority

» Get the sounds right.

» Build a weekly schedule you love

» Make a product that you're proud of

» Deliver a service that you're proud of

» Hire people that you like

THE PATRIOT WAY | CONSISTENCY IS KING

> "You have to go with the person who you have the most confidence in, the most consistent. And if it doesn't work, it doesn't work, but I'm going down with that person."
>
> — COACH BILL BELICHICK

If you own a business and want to experience the consistent winnings that Coach Bill Belichick experiences, take the following action steps:

» Schedule a reoccurring staff meeting at the same time every week.

» Schedule a group interview every week.

» Plan out your day. Every day.

» Schedule a weekly team training meeting.

THE PATRIOT WAY | HIS WINNING PERCENTAGE AS AN NFL HEAD COACH IS 76.8%

https://www.patriots.com/news/300-wins-amazing-stats-from-bill-belichick-s-career

COACH BILL BELICHICK FUN FACT #96

BILL BELICHICK IS NOT AFRAID TO CUT ANYBODY FROM HIS ROSTER

Coach Bill Belichick demonstrated time and time again that nobody had a secured roster spot that was 100% on the Patriots roster. Coach Bill Belichick believed that he needed to put the best players on the field that gave his team the best possible chance to win any given Sunday. Fan favorites in New England such as Terry Glenn & Drew Bledsoe were traded away because Coach Bill Belichick did not believe that they offered the team the best chance to win. In fact, during the 2003 season, Coach Bill Belichick decided to cut the long-time New England Patriots and seven-year veteran Lawyer Milloy at the very end of the team's training camp. At the time, ESPN commentator and analyst Tom Jackson reported that the Patriots team, "hate their coach." However, over time fans, players and the members of The Patriots organization began to accept and understand that constantly evolving the roster was going to be Coach Bill Belichick's normal. During Coach Bill Belichick's time as the head coach and general manager of The New England Patriots, Coach Bill Belichick trades away team stars such as Logan Mankins, Richard Seymour and Randy Moss because Coach Bill Belichick thought that the draft picks that he could acquire in return were actually worth more than the current players on his team. Although fans loved Vince Wilfork, Willie McGinest and Wes Welker, Coach Bill Belichick put his emotions aside and let these key players leave the team via free agency.

COACH BILL BELICHICK FUN FACT #97

COACH BILL BELICHICK IS CONSISTENTLY COUNTER-INTUITIVE

Coach Bill Belichick has been known for consistently trading highly valued top draft picks down in exchange for amassing more lower round draft picks. Under Coach Bill Belichick, the Patriots decided to transition into a pass-first offensive gameplan when the rest of the league was not trending in this direction. In order to move the Patriots into a pass first offense he aggressively drafted tight-ends Rob Gronkowski and the off the field troubled Aaron Hernandez during the 2010 National Football League Draft.

COACH BILL BELICHICK FUN FACT #98

COACH BILL BELICHICK WILL BENCH PLAYERS

Coach Bill Belichick earned a reputation over the years as a coach that will bench anyone. In fact, during the 2014 season, he decided to bench a running back by the name of Jonas Gray after Jonas Gray had just run for 201 yards against the Colts for oversleeping and then arriving late to the team's practice. Gray went on to only gain 256 yards over the remainder of his career. Coach Bill Belichick has also benched players for allowing sacks, fumbling during key situations and for throwing interceptions.

Coach Bill Belichick's most famous benching situation however involved Malcomb Butler and was not fully explained for years after the benching occurred. After playing Malcomb Butler at the position of cornerback during nearly every play for the majority of the Patriots regular season, and during each of the New England Patriots' first two playoff football games, Coach Bill Belichick decided to take the former Super Bowl hero and fan favorite out of the lineup for Super Bowl LII. During the game, Malcomb Butler played just one play on special teams during a game where the Philadelphia Eagles dominated offensively. During this game, Philadelphia's Nick Foles threw for a remarkable 373 passing yards while amassing three touchdowns in the stunning 41-33 upset.

Years passed and neither Coach Bill Belichick nor Malcomb Butler ever spoke about the benching that took place. However, writer Seth Wickersham reported in his book "It's Better to Be Feared" that Malcomb Butler was put on the bench after he had to be confronted by Patriots Coach Matt Patricia for demonstrating a lack of effort during practice.

> "I Joined Instaface."
> - COACH BILL BELICHICK
>
> "You get the job done or you don't."
> - COACH BILL BELICHICK

https://www.youtube.com/watch?v=GwkPcChwM98

COACH BILL BELICHICK WAS A MASTER GENERAL MANAGER

Coach Bill Belichick's ability to manage the personnel on his team and his salary cap management skills were known as being among the NFL's best. Under Coach Bill Belichick's leadership, the New England Patriots almost never signed contracts that the team ended up regretting while they were also able to keep around players that they wanted more often than not. Under Coach Bill Belichick's leadership skills, The New England Patriots were able to move forward with EPIC successful trades for veterans such as wide receiver, Randy Moss and running back, Corey Dillon. Coach Bill Belichick insisted that the stars he recruited had to take pay cuts in order to join his team and they often were willing to do just that.

COACH BELICHICK HAS MADE TV & MOVIE APPEARANCES

Coach Bill Belichick made cameo appearances in the 2005 movie, "Rescue Me" and "The NFL on CBS." As the self-proclaimed "Number One Coach Bill Belichick" fan I believe that he should be presented with an honorary Oscar Award, Emmy Award, Grammy Award, Golden Globe Award, BET Hip Hop Award, an ESPY Award and a Pulitzer Peace Prize.

COACH BILL BELICHICK COULD TRANSITION INTO BECOMING A MEDIA MOGUL IF HE WANTED TO:

While still working as the official head coach of the New England Patriots in 2019, Coach Bill Belichick appeared as one of three leading analysts alongside host Rich Eisen and Cris Collinsworth, for the NFL 100 All-Time Team series which was shown on the NFL Network. Coach Bill Belichick was selected due to his vast and always expanding knowledge of the current football landscape and football history. Coach Bill Belichick was awarded a Sports Emmy in 2021 for his contributions and if there is any justice in the world he should be given the key to the city of Hollywood. I often describe Coach Bill Belichick as a mix between Leonardo DiCaprio, William Shakespear, Steve Spielberg, Charlton Heston and Elvis during his peak performing years.

COACH BILL BELICHICK IS A WALKING & TALKING NOTABLE QUOTABLE MACHINE

"To live in the past is to die in the present."
- COACH BILL BELICHICK

"I'm not really worried about the other 31 teams."
- COACH BILL BELICHICK

"Things happen so quickly. We don't have time for one person to tell everybody what to do. Everybody needs to know what to do in those situations."
- COACH BILL BELICHICK

"Whatever success I've had is because I've tried to understand the situation of the player. I think the coach's duty is to avoid complicating matters."
- COACH BILL BELICHICK

"A lot of performance is based on confidence, knowing what you're doing, and being familiar, and not thinking too much and trying to play at confident game speed."
- COACH BILL BELICHICK

"If you sit back & spend too much time feeling good about what you did in the past, you're going to come up short next time."
- COACH BILL BELICHICK

"For a team to accomplish their goals, everybody's gotta give up a little bit of their individuality."
- COACH BILL BELICHICK

WHY BILL BELICHICK?

Listeners of the Thrivetime Radio Show and "Thrivers" (members of the Thrive15.com entrepreneurial community) often ask me why am I so obsessed with head coach, Coach Bill Belichick. I'm not from Boston, I'm not a shameless apologist for Boston Sports, my businesses are not based in Boston, and I have no family members that live in Boston so that's really a fair question. So why do I constantly reference Coach Bill Belichick when teaching best-practice management systems to business owners? And the answer is....

I love to study proven and consistent long-term winners in all walks of life so that I can apply their proven strategies, methods, and mindsets to my own life and businesses. I have found that coaching an NFL team is very similar to running a business in America. The National Football League is one of America's most competitive professional sports leagues and if the team doesn't win, the head coach gets fired. Sound familiar? In the world of business, if your team does not produce a profit, the owner or manager gets fired. The National Football League is filled with rules that are intentionally designed to create parody yet, Coach Bill Belichick just keeps on winning. The American government has also created rules that are been designed to create parody in our economy. With our current tax system (as of pre-2017), the more you make, the more the government takes in taxes. In the NFL, every team has to stick within a salary cap (an annual budget) and the head coach must produce victories (profits) or the head coach (boss) gets fired. Each year in the NFL, the team that wins the Super Bowl is then rewarded with the most difficult playing schedule in the league and the worst draft picks in the next National Football League Draft. Having been self-employed for 28 years, I know that this is exactly like running a business. In business, you work as hard as possible to create a positive, winning, and profitable business and then once you do, all of your competitors are aiming for you and offering your top talent top salaries to leave your team and to go play for them.

In a league that is designed to not create sustainable dynasties, Coach Bill Belichick just keeps on winning. Every year, he invests the time needed to discover the strengths of the players and the weaknesses of his opponents so that he can win with the team that he has. In the world of business, you and I must find a way to play and win with the players that we have. Coach Bill Belichick has created a culture where winning is expected in an organization that had lost consistently before he had arrived.

Coach Bill Belichick has turned his winning into a repeatable system that works year after year. You and I must do the same thing in the world of business. Throughout the course of this book, my goal is to look under the legendary, old, and beat up hoodies that Belichick is infamous for wearing and to give you a detailed look at the winning methods, processes, and strategies he uses to win year after year. You will be able to learn and apply these same principles and strategies into your own life and business. From personal experience, I can tell you this: once you learn to manage like Belichick, you will win in business.

CHAPTER ONE

HIRE CHARACTER & TRAIN SKILL

NOTABLE QUOTABLE

"Talent sets the floor. Character sets the ceiling."
Coach Bill Belichick

FUN FACTS

Coach Bill Belichick was born in Nashville, Tennessee, in the year of 1952. Bill landed his entrance into the NFL after graduating from Wesleyan in 1975. Belichick took the job with the NFL's Baltimore Colts for only $25 a week. He served as a gopher for head coach, Ted Marchibroda. Essentially, he did whatever the coach wanted him to do.

HOW TO APPLY THIS
PRINCIPLE IN YOUR BUSINESS

In your business, commit to recruiting character and training skill when possible.

CHAPTER TWO

BUILD YOUR SUCCESS BASED ON REPEATABLE SYSTEMS & NOT INDIVIDUAL TALENTS

NOTABLE QUOTABLE

"There is an old saying about the strength of the wolf is the pack, and I think there is a lot of truth to that. On a football team, it's not the strength of the individual players, but it is the strength of the unit and how they all function together."

Coach Bill Belichick

FUN FACTS

After landing his first job with the Baltimore Colts, Bill bounced all around the league. He joined a number of NFL teams including the Denver Broncos and the Detroit Lions. In the 1980s, Bill became the defensive coordinator for the New York Giants football team. During his time there, he was praised for being one of the most well-prepared and sharpest minds in the NFL. Belichick stayed with the Giants for 12 seasons. He eventually took over as the team's defensive coordinator under the legendary, Bill Parcells. Together, they coached the team to two Super Bowl victories.

HOW TO APPLY THIS PRINCIPLE IN YOUR BUSINESS

Make sure to build your business based upon the strength of your systems and not the unique unicorn talents of diva employees or you will find yourself constantly moving from feast to famine mode as employees come and go.

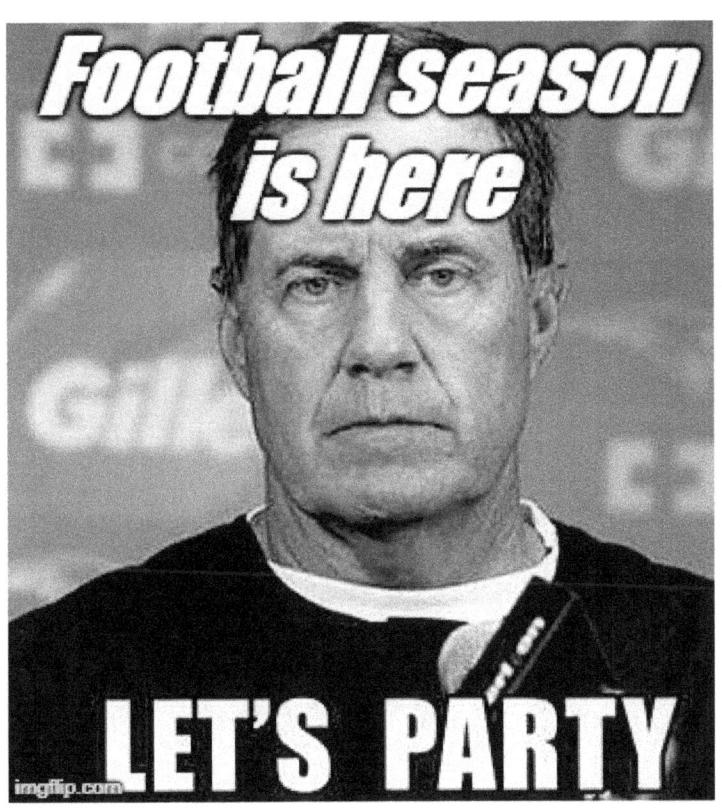

CHAPTER
THREE

DO THE
RIGHT
THING
FOR THE TEAM

NOTABLE QUOTABLE

"Mental toughness is doing the right thing for the team when it's not the best thing for you."
Coach Bill Belichick

FUN FACTS

Once the Giants had won their second Super Bowl, other NFL teams began to pursue Coach Bill Belichick to become their head coach. The Cleveland Browns owner, Art Modell, reached out to Belichick and eventually hired him to be their new head coach. During Bill's time in Cleveland, things were not good. He was very demanding of his players and he had little support from the upper management. His interviews with the local media did not help his case either. The combination of perpetually losing and not being loved by the media ultimately cost him his job. After the 1995 season, Art Modell announced that he was moving the franchise to Baltimore and that Coach Bill Belichick was fired. The management never gave Bill the control over the team and he was never able to win over the full support of the management.

HOW TO APPLY THIS
PRINCIPLE IN YOUR BUSINESS

To win in business, you must win with The 3 Ps: a PRODUCT or SERVICE that your customers love, PROFITS that feed your family, and quality PEOPLE who you enjoy working with.

CHAPTER FOUR

DON'T ALLOW YOURSELF OR YOUR TEAM TO BE DISTRACTED

NOTABLE QUOTABLE

"I don't Twitter, I don't MyFace, I don't Yearbook."
Coach Bill Belichick

FUN FACT

"Employers, be prepared for alarm as you review the newest statistical breakdown: 31% of employees waste roughly 30 minutes daily. 31% of employees waste roughly 1 hour daily. 16% of employees waste roughly 2 hours daily. 6% of employees waste roughly 3 hours daily. 2% of employees waste roughly 4 hours daily. 2% of employees waste 5 or more hours daily."

- This is according to an article that appeared in Forbes called, Wasting Time at Work - The Epidemic Continues.

FUN FACT

EA Sports, which produces the Madden series of NFL games, has a licensing contract with the NFL Coaches Association. It pays the NFLCA for the use of the coaches' likeness or name. EA Sports then pays the NFLCA and then they turn around and pay out to their members. The only NFL head coach that does not receive a portion of the revenue is Coach Bill Belichick. This is because he refuses to become a member of the NFL Coaches Association. If he signed up, he would get paid, but he refuses to join because he is obsessed with minimizing distractions.

FUN FACT

....

After being fired, he was able to find work quickly with his mentor, Bill Parcells. Parcells was the head coach of the New England Patriots at the time. Bill and Bill coached together in New England for the 1996 season and during that same year, the New England Patriots made it to the Super Bowl, where they ultimately lost to the Green Bay Packers. The year after their Super Bowl appearance, Belichick was invited to follow Parcells to the New York Jets, where Parcells had been hired as the new head coach.

HOW TO APPLY THIS
PRINCIPLE IN YOUR BUSINESS

....

As a manager, you must make sure that you and your team are focused on winning. Don't focus on looking good on Facebook, Linkedin, Youtube, Twitter, and other social media platforms because they will not produce results for your company during the work day.

CHAPTER FIVE

HAVE A BIAS FOR RESULTS

NOTABLE QUOTABLE

"You get the job done or you don't."
Coach Bill Belichick

FUN FACT

In 2000, the New England Patriots and their owner, Bob Kraft, decided to hire Belichick. Since being named as the team's head coach, he has guided the franchise to four Super Bowl victories.

HOW TO APPLY THIS
PRINCIPLE IN YOUR BUSINESS

Coach Bill Belichick unemotionally manages his roster based upon the performance and versatility of the player, and you should too. As an NFL coach, a business owner, or manager, we must produce a profit and operate within a budget.

CHAPTER
SIX

MAKE INTERNAL TRAINING DIFFICULT ON YOUR TEAM

NOTABLE QUOTABLE

"My personal coaching philosophy, my mentality, has always been to make things as difficult as possible for players in practice, however bad we can make them, I make them."

Coach Bill Belichick

FUN FACT

After a challenging 2000 season, Belichick made the difficult decision to replace the team's current All Pro and local fan favorite, Drew Bledsoe, with an unknown player by the name of Tom Brady. Brady played college football at the University of Michigan and was drafted by the Patriots in the sixth round of the 2000 NFL Draft.

HOW TO APPLY THIS
PRINCIPLE IN YOUR BUSINESS

As a manager and business owner, you must set high expectations for your team that are far higher than the expectations of your customers (fans). When you do that, you will win.

NOTABLE QUOTABLE

....

"Be a yardstick of quality. Some people aren't used to an environment where excellence is expected."

- Steve Jobs
(The co-founder of Apple and the former CEO of PIXAR)

CHAPTER SEVEN

PLAY SMART AND HARD

NOTABLE QUOTABLE

"You can play hard. You can play aggressive. You can give 120%, but if one guy is out of position then someone is running through the line of scrimmage and he is going to gain a bunch of yards."

Coach Bill Belichick

FUN FACT

During his time as the head coach of the New England Patriots, Belichick was named "Coach of the Year" three times. He was named "Coach of the Year" in 2003, 2007, and 2010. In the years of 2007 and 2011, Bill coached the New England Patriots to the Super Bowl, where they lost (both times) to Eli Manning and the New York Giants.

HOW TO APPLY THIS PRINCIPLE IN YOUR BUSINESS

You must make sure that your systems and processes are as efficient as possible so that you can operate as efficiently as possible. If you don't do this, you will lose no matter how hard everybody in your organization is working.

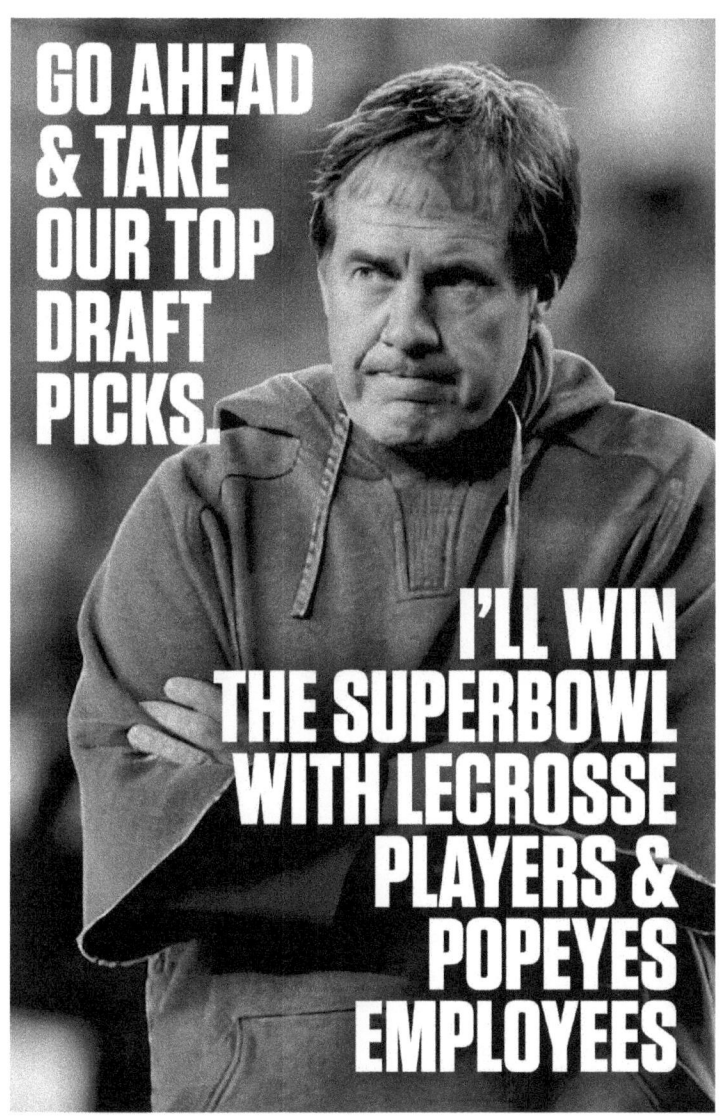

CHAPTER EIGHT

UNDERSTAND THE STRENGTHS & WEAKNESSES OF EACH TEAM MEMBER

NOTABLE QUOTABLE

"I think a smart guy can learn. Some guys learn - it's just like all of us - some guys can learn electronics, some of us can't. Some people can learn something else, some of us can't. I mean, we're all wired differently."

Coach Bill Belichick

FUN FACT

In 2007, Coach Belichick became the first head coach in the history of the NFL to coach a team to an undefeated 16-0 regular season record.

HOW TO APPLY THIS
PRINCIPLE IN YOUR BUSINESS

Management is all about putting your team members in positions where they can perform at their highest and best level. In the world of business, you must be candid with yourself and your team about the capacities and God-given talents that they have. If you don't, you will end up putting members of your team in positions where they are not able to perform at their peak.

CHAPTER NINE

PUT YOUR TEAM MEMBERS IN A POSITION TO PERFORM AT THEIR PEAK

NOTABLE QUOTABLE

"Some guys are football smart and they're not smart in other ways. Other guys get 1500 on their SATs and can't get a double-team block right. No, that definitely - in my experience, sometimes it correlates, sometimes it doesn't. I don't think you just take it for granted."

Coach Bill Belichick

FUN FACT

During the 2014 season, Belichick tied the NFL coaching records. He guided the team to its sixth appearance in the Super Bowl and its fourth NFL championship.

HOW TO APPLY THIS
PRINCIPLE IN YOUR BUSINESS

In the world of business, degrees and resumes don't matter but results do. As a manager, you must put the team members in your office that can deliver the best results regardless of their background.

FUN FACT

THIS IS AN ABBREVIATED LIST OF UNDRAFTED DIFFERENCE MAKERS THAT HAVE BEEN RECRUITED BY BELICHICK DURING HIS TIME AS THE HEAD COACH OF THE PATRIOTS.

Adam Vinatieri - He's the best field goal kicker of his generation and he was not drafted after playing his college career at South Dakota State.

Lonie Paxton - The long-snapper was undrafted in 2000 and yet was signed by the Patriots. He was important during many key moments.

Wes Welker - After having a good career at Texas Tech, he was not drafted. The Chargers signed him, but he was cut. He then played for the Dolphins for two years before joining the Patriots in 2007.

BenJarvus Green-Ellis - The Patriot with the super-long name played college at Ole Miss and went undrafted in 2008. He was signed by the Patriots and was a backup for many running backs until injuries created an opportunity for Green-Ellis to showcase his talents.

Stephen Neal - This man was a college wrestling champion who never even played college football at Cal-State Bakersfield. However, he showed that he had the skills needed to be a successful NFL offensive lineman. The Patriots signed him and he went on to become a solid team member for seven years.

And the list goes on...

CHAPTER TEN

VALUE RESULTS OVER TENURE

NOTABLE QUOTABLE

"We like to say that dependability is more important than ability."

Coach Bill Belichick

FUN FACT

In 2007, it was exposed that the New England Patriots had secretly video-taped opposing coaches. This incident is infamously now known as Spygate. As a result of this incident, Coach Belichick was fined $500,000 by the National Football League. In 2008, the New England Patriots were fined again. This time they were fined $250,000 and they lost a first-round draft pick for the 2008 NFL draft. In 2014, the NFL launched a special investigation as to whether Coach Belichick directed the team's equipment managers to under inflate footballs in the 2014 AFC title game.

HOW TO APPLY THIS
PRINCIPLE IN YOUR BUSINESS

As a manager, you can't manage people who don't consistently come to work. Get rid of people who can't find a way to get work consistently or you will lose as a result of your compassion.

CHAPTER ELEVEN

GIVE A CHANCE TO UNPROVEN TALENT

NOTABLE QUOTABLE

"I think Tom is one of the most consistent players that I've ever coached. He works hard every week. There are no ups and downs with him."

Coach Bill Belichick

FUN FACT

Tom Brady was drafted by the Patriots in the sixth round of the 2000 NFL draft. He initially found himself as the team's fourth quarterback on the depth chart and as a player fighting for a roster spot. As a result of diligence, he moved up to become the Patriots' backup quarterback. Unfortunately, he only played one game during his first NFL season. During the 2001 season, the team's starting All-Pro quarterback, Drew Bledsoe, was injured and Brady quickly proved himself to be the perfect man for the job. He lead the team to 11 wins and 3 losses during the 14 games he played. In the post-season, he lead the team to a win over the St. Louis Rams during Super Bowl XXXVI. He was named the Most Valuable Player of the Super Bowl.

HOW TO APPLY THIS
PRINCIPLE IN YOUR BUSINESS

As a manager, you must surround yourself with consistent performers who don't have massive emotional ups and downs or you will have a dramatic office environment filled with turmoil. You must develop a bias for consistent and diligent performers.

CHAPTER TWELVE

FOCUS ON RESULTS, NOT TENURE

NOTABLE QUOTABLE

"To live in the past is to die in the present."

Coach Bill Belichick

FUN FACT

Drew Bledsoe had just been signed to a 10 year contract whenever he was injured during a football game. He suffered from a sheared blood vessel in his chest. Coach Bill Belichick replaced him with the team's back-up, Tom Brady.

HOW TO APPLY THIS PRINCIPLE IN YOUR BUSINESS

As a successful manager, you should not promote people based upon tenure, but rather, you should promote people based upon the results that they deliver in the workplace. If you promote people and provide them with raises based solely on tenure, you will create a business that begins to operate with the efficiency of a government or organization...which is not good.

CHAPTER THIRTEEN

BE CANDID WITH YOUR TEAM

NOTABLE QUOTABLE

"This won't be good enough. It wasn't good enough today. It won't be good enough against anybody else, either."

Coach Bill Belichick

FUN FACT

During the mid-2004 season, the New England Patriots' secondary was filled with injuries. The Super Bowl XXXVIII starters, Tyrone Poole and Ty Law, were both injured for the remainder of the season so it was on the undrafted rookie, Randall Gay, and team's second-year cornerback, Asante Samuel, to deliver. The team also needed a third member of the secondary. Belichick elected to use the team's star receiver, Troy Brown, to fill in as the slot cornerback. Brown made a huge impact for the team while in this position. He even made an interception from his former quarterback, Drew Bledsoe.

HOW TO APPLY THIS
PRINCIPLE IN YOUR BUSINESS

As a manager, you must be candid with your team about where they stand, and how well or poor they are performing on the job. Whatever you accept, you must expect. Set high expectations and push your team to perform at a high level and you will win.

CHAPTER FOURTEEN

DON'T ALLOW BAD HABITS TO INFECT YOUR TEAM

NOTABLE QUOTABLE

"One thing that could be a problem is breaking old habits. It's not that you don't understand what the new responsibilities or plays are, but just the fact that you've been doing something a long time and you're kind of used to doing it, it's a habit, and that's not what's required in the other system and that means kind of undoing something before you can even start to do something new."

Coach Bill Belichick

FUN FACT

In 2002, Belichick elected to begin using the solid defensive player, Mike Vrabel, on offense as tight-end during goal-line situations. During the next five seasons and throughout the playoffs, Vrabel scored eight touchdowns.

HOW TO APPLY THIS
PRINCIPLE IN YOUR BUSINESS

Beware of paying a premium price for hiring experienced people who bring bad habits into the workplace. Regardless of their age only hire coachable and trainable people or you will end up with a team of people running around and making excusing while proclaiming, "well that isn't the way they taught me to do it at my last job."

CHAPTER
FIFTEEN

INSIST ON MANIACAL PREPARATION

NOTABLE QUOTABLE

"I think practice preparation is always an indicator of game performance - not necessarily 100 percent, because there are still a lot of variables there, but it's still an indicator."

Coach Bill Belichick

FUN FACT

Coach Bill Belichick is committed to winning year after year and to making the tough calls that other NFL coaches or managers wouldn't be willing to do. After winning the Superbowl, Bill decided to release the team's captain, Lawyer Milloy. At the time of the cut, Belichick commented that had been the hardest release he'd ever had to make. Milloy was 29 years old, a fan favorite, and the heart and soul of the Patriots locker room. The decision was made on September 2nd, 2003, the morning before New England's scheduled season opener to be played against the Buffalo Bills. The cut shook up members of the team. ESPN and NFL analyst, Tom Jackson, described the Patriots locker room by saying, "they hate their coach." Milloy quickly scored a job with the Buffalo Bills and he played a key role in the Buffalo's 31-0 win over New England. However, as the year went on, Belichick was once again proven to be right. The Patriots' new pickup Pro Bowl safety, Rodney Harrison, proved to be able to produce the same results on the field as Milloy but at much less of a cost.

HOW TO APPLY THIS
PRINCIPLE IN YOUR BUSINESS

Push your team harder when you are coaching and training them than your customers will push them. You must have higher internal standards and expectations for your team than your customers will have for them.

CHAPTER SIXTEEN

BUILD A VERSATILE TEAM

NOTABLE QUOTABLE

"A lot of times a player has a lot of versatility. That's really what their strength is and what their role is."

Coach Bill Belichick

FUN FACT

Coach Bill Belichick is one of the few head coaches in the NFL who has gone without coordinators. Belichick prefers to keep his coaching staff very small, and has chosen to go without offensive or defensive coordinators routinely in the past. As an example, in the year 2000, Belichick decided to go without a defensive coordinator. His defensive staff did include Brian Daboll, Eric Mangini, and Rob Ryan. In 2005, after he lost his offensive coordinator, Charlie Weis. Belichick named the unproven 29-year-old quarterbacks coach, Josh McDaniels, as the Patriots offensive play-caller. It was not until the following season that he named McDaniels as the team's offensive coordinator. When McDaniels left to take the head coaching job in Denver, his replacement, Bill O'Brien, was not named as the team's offensive coordinator until his second season in this role as well.

HOW TO APPLY THIS
PRINCIPLE IN YOUR BUSINESS

As a manager, you never want to hire someone who says, "that's not my job." You must build a winning team based upon a culture of people who are willing to do whatever it takes to win and who are willing to learn new job skills everyday.

CHAPTER SEVENTEEN

MORE BILL BELICHICK FUN FACTS

1. Belichick's father, Steve, started out volunteering and then working as the equipment manager for the Detroit Lions to actually playing for the team in 1941.

2. After serving in World War II, Belichick began coaching football professionally. He started out as the head football coach and the head basketball coach at Hiram College. He worked as an assistant coach for Vanderbilt University (1949–1952), the University of North Carolina at Chapel Hill (1953–1955), and then as an assistant coach for the United States Naval Academy for 34 years.

3. While in high school Coach Bill Belichick played lacrosse and football, but preferred lacrosse.

4.   Coach Bill Belichick graduated from Annapolis High School in 1970.

5. After graduating from High School, Bill spent one year of his life at the Phillips Academy in Andover, Massachusetts.

6.   Coach Bill Belichick went to college at Wesleyan University in Middletown, Connecticut.

7. Belichick played tight end and center on the Wesleyan football team.

8. Coach Bill Belichick graduated from Wesleyan University with a degree in economics in 1975.

9. Coach Bill Belichick spent 10 years working in entry level coaching positions for the Baltimore Colts, the Detroit Lions, the Denver Broncos and the New York Giants before he finally scored the defensive coordinator job with the giants in 1985.

10. Coach Bill Belichick has been an assistant or head coach with the following franchises:
    - The Baltimore Colts
    - The Cleveland Browns
    - The Denver Broncos
    - The Detroit Lions
    - The New England Patriots
    - The New York Giants
    - The New York Jets

11. Coach Bill Belichick is the only coach in the NFL who refuses to become a member of the National Football Coaches Association, which is why he does not share in any of the earnings produced from the games' sales and why you will not be able to find him, his playbook or any likenesses of him on any of the popular Madden video games.

12. Belichick changes the name of his boat every time the Patriots win a Super Bowl from "III Rings" to "IV Rings," etc.

ACTION ITEMS

Pass on what you've learned by writing a Google Review. Type in "Thrive15 Jenks" and write that review today!

Don't miss a radio show or podcast by subscribing on iTunes at ThriveTimeShow.com.

Get all of the interactive downloadables by signing up today at Thrive15.com.

WANT MORE?

Check out the Ultimate Textbook for Starting, Running & Growing Your Own Business!

How to Build a Successful Business

NEVER before has entrepreneurship been delivered in an UNFILTERED, real and raw way... until now. This book is NOT for people that want a politically correct and silver-lined happy-go-lucky view of entrepreneurship. That's crap. Supported by case studies and testimonials from entrepreneurs that have grown their businesses all over the planet using these best practice systems, former U.S. Small Business Administration Entrepreneur of the Year, Clay Clark, shares the specific action steps for successful business systems, hilarious stories from situations that every entrepreneur faces, and entrepreneurship factoids that are guaranteed to blow your mind.

JOIN US AT THE WORLD'S BEST 2-DAY INTENSIVE BUSINESS WORKSHOP

Get specific and practical training on how to grow your business

www.ingramcontent.com/pod-product-compliance
Lightning Source LLC
Chambersburg PA
CBHW051620120626
46551CB00014B/1881